SELF-ESTEEM WORKBOOK

WHY YOU ARE A BADASS

Discover the Secrets To Gaining Self-Confidence, Respect, and True Happiness In Life

TAYLOR DAUNT

Table of Contents

PART I 11

Chapter 1: Self-Esteem and Valuing Yourself........................ 12

How Low Self-Esteem Is Developed..14

The Different Types of Parents...14

Bullying 15

Trauma...17

The Science of Self-Esteem...19

Chapter 2: How You Can Matter to Yourself.......................... 21

How to Build Self-Awareness..22

Recognize What Bothers You About Other People............22

Meditate on Your Mind 23

Draw a Timeline of Your Life...24

Identify Your Emotional Kryptonite 24

Travel and Get Out a Little Bit..25

Pick Up a New Skill...25

Clarify Your True Values 26

Chapter 3: Creating a Stronger Self...28

Managing Your Ego 28

Don't Take Things Personally...29

Accepts All of Your Mistakes...29

Stop Being Self-Conscious 29

Realize That Your Ego Will Never Go Away 31

You Are Not the Best...31

Imagine Your Ego as Another Person 31

Stop Bragging...32

Be Grateful for the Little Things 32

Learn to Compliment Others 32

Forgiving People..33

Overcoming Trauma...36

Chapter 4: Changing Our Minds 39

How To Ignore Things..39

Stop Comparing Yourself To Others 39

Ignore Societal Pressure 40

Start Living In The Present Moment............................41

Leverage Your Purpose...41

The Mindset Shift 42

Now That Your Self-Esteem is High.............................43

PART II 46

Chapter 1: Self-Confidence In Various Situations 47

How a Lack of Self-Confidence Affects Us 48

Chapter 2: Social Anxiety...50

Social Anxiety and Lack of Confidence In Specific Situations 51

Chapter 3: Learning to Become Comfortable..........56

Building Your Self-Confidence......................................56

Groom Yourself Regularly 57

Photoshop Your Self-Image..57

Destroy Negative Thoughts 57

Get to Know Yourself 58

Be Kind and Generous 58

Be Prepared 58

Know Your Principles and Live By Them.............................59

Speak Slowly...59

Stand Up Straight...60

Increase Your Competence Levels.....................................60

Set Small Goals and Achieve Them....................................60

Change Small Habits About Yourself..................................60

Focus Your Attention on Solutions....................................61

Become Active..61

Gain More Knowledge..61

Overcoming Procrastination...62

Build Confidence At Work...64

Chapter 4: Getting Rid of Social Anxiety.........................67

Chapter 1: Self-Care Is the Best Care............................72

How Does Self-Care Work...73

How Does Self-Care Improve Self-Esteem and Self-Confidence?.....74

Chapter 2: What Does Good Self-Care Look Like?...............77

Good Self-Care Practices...77

Taking Responsibility for Your Happiness............................77

You Become Assertive With Others....................................77

You Treat Yourself As You Would a Close Friend.....................77

You Are Not Afraid to Ask for What You Want.......................78

Your Life Is Set Around Your Own Values............................78

Chapter 3: Demanding Your Own Self-Care.......................79

Setting Healthy Boundaries...79

Identify and Name Your Limits...79

Stay Tuned Into Your Feelings...80

Don't Be Afraid of Being Direct 80

Give Yourself Permission to Set Boundaries 80

Consider Your Past and Present 81

Be Assertive 81

Start Small 81

Eliminating Toxicity and Not Caring About Losing Friends 82

Don't Expect People to Change 82

Establish and Maintain Boundaries 82

Don't Keep Falling for Crisis Situations 83

Focus on the Solution 83

Accept Your Own Difficulties and Weaknesses 83

They Won't Go Easily 83

Choose Your Battles Carefully 84

Surround Yourself With Healthy relationships 84

How to Focus on Self-Care 84

Pay Attention to Your Sleep 84

Take Care of Your Gut 85

Exercise and Physical Activity Is Essential 85

Consider a Mediterranean Diet 85

Take a Self-Care Trip 86

Get Outside 86

Bring a Pet Into Your Life 86

Get Yourself Organized 86

Cook Yourself Meals At Home 87

Read Regularly 87

Schedule Your Self-Care Time 87

Chapter 4: How to Be Happy Being Alone 88

Accept Some Alone Time..88

Do Not Compare Yourself to Others....................................88

Step Away From Social Media..88

Take a Break From Your Phone...89

Allow Time for Your Mind to Wander..................................89

Take Yourself on a Date...89

Exercise...89

Take Advantage of the Perks of Being Alone.......................89

Find a Creative Outlet..90

Take Time to Self-Reflect...90

Make Plans for Your Future...90

Make Plans for Solo Outings...90

Chapter 1: Back to the Basics...93

Chapter 2: Unlocking Your True Purpose Through Mindfulness.............97

Re-centering Yourself...97

Giving Your Emotions Space...99

Making Clear Decisions...100

Keeping Yourself Safe...100

Improving Relationships..101

Fostering True Joy...103

Chapter 3: Moving Mindfully in Daily Life.........................105

Coming to the Present Moment: Daily Guided Mindfulness Meditation
With Journaling (Week 1)..105

Coming to the Present Moment: Daily Guided Mindfulness Meditation
With Journaling (Week 2)..109

Coming to the Present Moment: Daily Guided Mindfulness Meditation
With Journaling (Week 3)..111

Mini Meditation Toolbox: 15 Quick and Easy Meditations to Integrate
Mindfulness Into Your Daily Life..114

Mini Meditation Toolbox: 10 Quick and Easy Meditations to Ease Stress, Depression, Addiction, Anxiety, Pain, Distraction, and Loss Using Mindfulness 123

Chapter 1: Is This for You?..131

Chapter 2: Your Toolbox, DBT 133

Chapter 3: Finding Yourself through Mindfulness 138

Chapter 4: Taking Mindfulness to the Next Level with Advanced Meditation Techniques 142

Chapter 5: Using Your New Tools to Process Negative Emotions 147

Chapter 6: Defining Your Goals, Your Values, and Yourself.................151

Chapter 7: Living in the Positive! 154

Chapter 8: How DBT Has Enhanced Your Life 158

PART I

Chapter 1: Self-Esteem and Valuing Yourself

Imagine waking up in the morning and being full of life. You are energetic as you get out of bed and are ready to attack the day because nothing can stop you. Any type of challenge that comes your way, you are prepared to face it head-on and overcome it. You take pride in your work and relationships because you understand their worth. You also understand the value that you bring to the day, so you carry yourself with strength and dignity.

On the other hand, picture yourself waking up in a crummy mood. You are not looking forward to the day ahead, and no matter what good things may come, they are quickly tossed aside, and your mind wanders towards the negative side. You suffer from anxiety throughout the day, and you avoid any challenging situation you can because you lack faith in yourself.

These two mindsets are entirely different from one another, but they are related to the same thing: Your self-esteem. Self-esteem is the amount of respect that you place on yourself. It is how much you value your skills and ability to handle life and all its circumstances. Those who place a high value on themselves have a high level of self-esteem. Those who set a low value on themselves suffer from low self-esteem.

Your self-esteem is also your self-worth, and you mustn't put a low price tag on your abilities.

Having high self-esteem does not mean you ignore your flaws. It means that you love yourself despite all of them. You recognize your weaknesses, and therefore, are more likely to fix them. In the end, you love yourself because of your own self-beliefs.

As we grow up, we are constantly surrounded by things that affect our psyche. Our ego is the part of our mind that has a direct relationship with the outside world. When we experience an event or interact with a specific individual, it will determine how we feel at that exact moment. If the situation is upsetting, then it can bring out a range of different emotions in us. For those who are dealing with low self-esteem, they will easily be triggered by an outside event. For example, if someone calls us a negative name, it might make us feel sad or angry. This one incident could ruin our whole day in an instant. If we are experiencing negativity over a long period of time, then these thoughts will slowly enter into our subconscious and unconscious mind, where they stay forever, unless we purposefully remove them.

If you have a healthy level of self-esteem, then these situations will roll off your back. Negative people or situations will not change the feelings you have towards yourself because you will be in complete control of your emotions. I am not suggesting that being insulted will not be hurtful for this type of individual, but they will understand how to manage it and not let it affect them negatively. They don't define themselves by other people's opinions.

I can talk all day about the extreme benefits of self-esteem, as there are many. The focus of this book, though, is how to develop and build your self-esteem, even if you have been suffering from low levels of it your whole life. I am working off the assumption that you are in the camp of low self-esteem. Therefore, you already know how it feels, because you are personally living it.

How Low Self-Esteem Is Developed

The first step in dealing with low self-esteem is recognizing that you have it. Now that we have established that, it is important to determine why you have low self-esteem.

The Different Types of Parents

One of the major contributing factors to our self-esteem is our parents and how they raised us. Our mother and father are generally the first people we become close to. How they interact with us will initially determine how we value ourselves. Even if a parent is loving, there are still specific tendencies that can be counterproductive to use raising our self-worth.

While parents often push their children to succeed, some can become overbearing to the point where they use ridicule, harsh criticisms, and even abuse to ensure their children stay on the straight path. While some parents do not have malicious intent when they become disapproving authority figures, others will purposefully look down on their kids and make them feel inferior. Children who grow up under these conditions grow into adults who are never comfortable in their own skin.

On the opposite end of the overbearing caregiver is the uninvolved caregiver who does not care one bit. They ignore their children as if they are not necessary. In fairness, this can often be done unintentionally. For example, the parents work so much and become excessively focused on their jobs. They are obsessed with making a living and ignore the people closest to them, including their children. When children get ignored by the influential adults in their lives, they become confused about their place in the world. They feel forgotten and unimportant, and therefore, they believe their existence to be bothersome to people.

Another parental issue that affects children is the parents or caregivers who are in constant conflict. When these adults fight and throw hurtful language at one another, especially in front of children, they absorb these negative emotions. These children can feel like they contributed to the fighting in some way. Growing into adulthood, these same children will feel like they are the cause of so many different conflicts, simply because they were nearby.

Bullying

Bullying has been an issue for children and adults alike for generations.

The powerful always seem to push around the weak. With children, this power is usually in the form of physical dominance. The bigger and stronger child picks on the smaller and weaker one. Of course, the bullying can be mental or psychological, too, if the child can pull it off.

Bullying can also become a significant contributor to low self-esteem. A child who is constantly bullied in any way will develop a poor self-image about themselves. Unfortunately, bullying will never go away. What matters in these situations is the support that children receive from their parents. The way the adults in a child's life handle the aftermath of bullying will play a major role in their mindset development.

Many children do not have a comforting environment to come home to, which is detrimental to their psyche. After experiencing abuse outside the come, they walk through their front door and experience even more of it. This makes a child feel worthless and abandoned. They become lost further into the abyss and think they do not belong anywhere. Having unsupportive parents will magnify the effects of bullying.

Furthermore, some parents were over-supportive. These are the ones who coddled their children and gave them no coping skills to deal with the outside world. As a result, they will be ill-prepared to deal with the cruel world that exists out there, which is not going away anytime soon. When children become adults and enter the real world, they will face some harsh criticisms that will challenge their beliefs about who they are. If they were always buttered up as children, they would not understand how to face rejection, insults, or people being mean to them.

No parent wants their children to feel bad, but they cannot be shielded from disappointment their whole lives. Once they do face this disappointment in the real world, they will fall apart because they have no actual self-worth. All of their value is tied to the compliments that other people give them.

I know I have been singling out parents here, and that's because they are the adults a child spends the most amount of time with. However, other adults, like extended family members, teachers, coaches, or counselors, can also do their part in providing a supportive atmosphere for the children in their lives.

Trauma

Trauma can be physical, emotional, or sexual, and no matter what kind you were a victim of, it will devastate your self-esteem, especially as a child. With trauma, you are being forced into a position against your will, which makes you feel like you've lost power and control of your situation.

Situations like this will make you feel worthless. You will even blame yourself for causing the trauma or abuse. This is a method many people use to gain control back into their lives. They believe that by taking the blame, they will be able to manage the situation the next time it comes around

Children do not have control over who is in their lives. This means they are often stuck in abusive situations and have no way of getting out of it. If they are lucky, someone will recognize it, and they will help them get out.

A child who goes through trauma will grow into an adult who is unsure of themselves in many ways. They will never feel like they are good enough, will always feel like they are to blame for specific situations, and will have a distrust for humanity in general.

I know I have spoken about a lack of trust throughout this book. A significant part of having self-esteem is being able to put your faith into the unknown. When you lack trust, this faith does not exist, and therefore, you will always be paranoid and never fully confident in any situation.

Now, think back on your life and determine the traumatic events you may have gone through. How did these affect your psyche at that moment? How you felt on the inside when these various circumstances occurred will help you understand if they contributed to a lack of self-esteem.

We went over these issues simply to help you recognize the underlying causes of the value you place on yourself. There is nothing we can do about these situations now, but we can learn from them and work on ways to overcome our mental blocks to positive self-esteem.

The Science of Self-Esteem

There has been a lot of research done on the genetic components of low self-esteem. While people can be born with certain levels of chemicals that influence their emotions and brain activity, there is no conclusive evidence that people are born with high or low self-esteem. Even twins who grew up in different environments were found to have different qualities related to their self-worth, even though various other personality traits were similar. As of now, environmental factors seem to play a much more significant role.

Of course, this does not mean that there is no scientific component to all of this. As we go through various life stages, our brain development occurs based on life experiences. The actions we take and the thoughts we create make numerous neural pathways in our brain and nervous system, which determine our future behavior. For example, if we continuously have negative feelings, our mind becomes wired in a certain way to produce these same thoughts in the future. As a result, you habitually think negatively in every situation you come across.

Now that we have established what low self-esteem is, our goal in the next chapter is to help you rewire your brain, so you can start living with high self-esteem.

Chapter 2: How You Can Matter to Yourself

"Confront the dark parts of yourself, and work to banish them with illumination and forgiveness. Your willingness to wrestle with your demons will cause your angels to sing."

-August Summer

Now that we know what self-esteem is, it is hard to deny the role it plays in our lives. Any type of pursuit, whether personal, professional, relationships, or health, will require you to place a high value on yourself; otherwise, you will never progress forward as you should. At this moment, I want you to recognize the past mistakes that brought you to where you are now, but also forgive yourself for them because you can do nothing to change the past. You can learn from it, though, and build a new future where you actually value yourself and the gifts you bring to the world.

In the previous chapter, we discussed the numerous causes of low self-esteem, many of which stem from our childhood. Since our mindset took a long time to develop, it will take extreme effort with several actionable steps to change and overcome this thought-process. We will now discuss some specific steps and practices over the next few chapters you can engage in to improve your mindset and build-up your self-esteem.

We will approach this subject from many different aspects, so they can be combined to improve how you habitually think about yourself. Think of your mind as a structure that is built to think a specific way. Now imagine having to rebuild many different parts of that structure to change your thoughts. This is what we will be doing with all of the action steps we will go over.

How to Build Self-Awareness

Self-awareness means having the ability to understand the way you think, feel, and behave. This is a necessary quality to have if you want to fix your self-esteem. It is the best way to recognize if your actions correlate with low self-esteem. Once you become self-aware, you will know yourself much better. The following are some significant strategies you can employ right away.

Recognize What Bothers You About Other People

What bothers us most about other people are often the same qualities that we possess. For example, if someone is naturally aggressive, we may dislike it; however, it is a trait that we have, as well. We all have aspects of our personality that are unflattering, and since we don't want to admit them, we will ignore them fully. Ignorance is not bliss in the long-run, and if we do not pay attention to our negative qualities, they will rear their ugly heads at the most inopportune time. The next time a person is bothering you, stop and ask yourself if they are displaying something that is a reflection of you. Do you recognize their personality when you look in the mirror?

Meditate on Your Mind

Mindful meditation is a great way to learn about your thoughts and how they work. One of the main reasons we lack self-awareness is because we are thinking so much that our thoughts completely take over. Proper meditation allows us to separate ourselves from these thoughts and recognize that they do not fully encompass who we are. Through mindful meditation practices, you have the ability to observe your thoughts without becoming attached to them. Therefore, it is easier to see which ones deserve our attention and which ones do not. The following are some simple steps to get you started on this practice.

- Get comfortable by finding a quiet place that is as free from distractions as possible.
- Sit up with your back straight and chest out. It does not matter if you are in a chair or sitting cross-legged on the floor. You may even lie down flat on the floor.
- Take in some deep breaths through your nose and then out slowly through your mouth or nose. You should be able to feel the breaths down into your abdomen. This will help you relax.
- Pay attention to the sounds of your breaths and their rhythmic patterns. When you inhale, imagine breathing in joy and peace. When you breathe out, imagine getting rid of the toxicity in your mind.

- When you notice your thoughts wandering away from your breaths, immediately focus them back to the center. Take in your immediate surroundings and be in your present state. Do not think of the past or worry about the future.
- Make this practice a habit and do it routinely. Some of the best practitioners of mindful meditation have been doing it for years, and are still learning better ways to improve. These are all great steps to get you started and reorganize your mind.

As a side note, meditation is not only useful for self-awareness. It can help with stress and anxiety, communication, better sleep, improved focus on your goals, and overall mental health. All of this will lead back to higher self-esteem. Start off with five minutes and then build yourself up to 20-30. You will be amazed at how much clarity you will have about yourself.

Draw a Timeline of Your Life

Sit down with a notepad and try to remember as much as you can from the time of birth to where you are now. Pay special attention to significant moments that had a big impact on your life and circumstances, whether positive or negative. This practice will allow you to see certain moments of your life in context, which will give you a better idea of who you are. You will realize a lot about yourself and gain much self-awareness.

Identify Your Emotional Kryptonite

Think about the emotions that you absolutely hate having and try to avoid. For example, some individuals hate feeling sad so much that they drown this emotion with alcohol. The problem is, negative emotions are a gateway into our souls. They are trying to tell us something in a discrete way. If we pay attention to them as they are happening, we will learn a lot about our situation. If you are sad often, pay attention to why so you can finally address it.

Travel and Get Out a Little Bit

We often become stuck in our own little box and forget that there is a big world out there. Micro-travel, which means traveling to new destinations that are local to us, is a great way to get you out of your comfort zone and try out a new routine. Take frequent short trips if you can, and even travel abroad if this is feasible. This will help you gain a lot of awareness for the world around you, as well as teach you a lot about yourself. Travel to new destinations, even nearby, will significantly raise our self-awareness.

Pick Up a New Skill

Just like with travel, learning a new skill will force us to think and act in new ways, thereby forcing us to increase our self-awareness. We all develop certain routines as we grow older, and it causes us to go into a comfort zone. The main problem here is that it creates a strong, narrow-mindedness. Being willing to start something as a beginner will cultivate a level of flexibility in our minds and thoughts. The new skill does not have to be related to your career. It can also be hobbies like playing the piano, sculpting, or dancing.

Clarify Your True Values

How often do you sit down and assess what your true values are? If you are like most people, probably very seldomly. We often get so caught up in daily life that we have very little time for self-reflection, especially on the important things in life. As a result, we end up chasing false goals and not living the type of life we want to. People become so worried about moving up the career ladder and buying the latest fancy car, that they forget what actually makes them happy. In your case, you may have followed a safe career path rather than focus on what your true calling was.

A great technique you can perform is to set aside some time on a weekly or monthly basis and think about your life and circumstances. Ask yourself why you think you are here and what your purpose in life is? Also, imagine what a fulfilling life would look like for you. Spend about 30 minutes every time you do this. A major part of self-awareness is recognizing what really matters to you. This practice will be a great way to come to this understanding.

We tend to get lost in the monotony of life. So, it is important to practice these self-awareness techniques on a regular basis. Taking notice of your thoughts, behaviors, and actions in real-time is a special skill to have. It will go a long way in helping you build your self-esteem.

Chapter 3: Creating a Stronger Self

Going along the path of improved self-esteem, I will now discuss various strategies to strengthen your psyche. High self-esteem requires a strong mindset.

Managing Your Ego

I spoke briefly in chapter one about the ego. Our ego is basically our mind's direct connection to the outside world. What our environment gives, our ego responds. This means that whatever activities are going on around will make you feel a certain way, and this is directly the result based on how our ego responds. For example, if someone outshines us in some way, our ego will respond by making us feel inferior.

People who are not careful will have this aspect of the mind completely control them. As a result, the values they place on themselves are based on what the world thinks of them, rather than what they think of themselves. Every one of us has an ego to a certain degree, but the key is to not let it control us. We must learn to manage it properly so that our self-worth comes from within, rather than from what we can't control. The following are specific steps you can take to begin managing your ego so that it doesn't control you.

Don't Take Things Personally

Taking things too personally or literally can make you overthink and cause your mind to become infected. It's important to be at peace with yourself and realize that people do not always mean what they say. They are often angry or suffering from some other negative emotion. Even if they do mean it, people who treat others poorly have a problem within themselves, and not necessarily other people. In a moment where you are facing harsh words or actions, imagine your spot being replaced by someone else and watching the same people act in the same manner because, in most cases, they would. A big part of self-esteem is not caring what others think. This is a major step in that direction.

Accepts All of Your Mistakes

Accepting your mistakes, no matter how big or small is a positive way to work on your ego problems. Everyone makes mistakes, so there is no use in hiding them. Once you admit them, apologize, and move on, they no longer have control over you as you've released them from your psyche. Genuinely apologizing to someone is a great way to put your ego in check and grow as a person.

Stop Being Self-Conscious

Our ego prevents us from looking silly or goofy. We are so afraid of what others are thinking that we never let out guard down. This is a real definition of living in fear. If you have been acting this way for a while, then it's time to stop putting up a shield, and just let your silly self come out. You will actually be happier in the long run because showcasing your true self will attract your real friends. To stop being so self-conscious, try using the following steps.

- Shrug away your negative thoughts. This does not mean you should ignore them. Acknowledge that they are there, but then do not agree with them in any way.

- Don't put other people on pedestals. We have a tendency to do this, especially to those who we admire. Realize that they are regular people and not someone to bow down to.

- Think of a moment where you were self-conscious, and then imagine replacing yourself with someone you cared about in the position. If they felt the same way you did, then what would you tell them. Now, tell that same thing to yourself. We are often bigger critics of ourselves than we are other people.

- Accept yourself, with your faults and all. Remember that nobody is perfect, and if you want to gain a high level of self-esteem, then you must learn to love yourself, including your flaws.

- People are not paying as much attention to you as you may think. Part of our ego tells us that people are watching us and critiquing our every move. Understand that people are in their own world much of the time, and too busy in their personal self-doubts to pay attention to anyone else. Believe it or not, you are not the focus of attention all the time.

- Go do the thing that makes you self-conscious or nervous. Face it head-on, and you will realize it's not as bad as you may think. Do not let your awkwardness keep you on the sidelines. Jump in with both feet and dare to look foolish. If you hate dancing in front of people, join a dance class and do it several times a week. If you suck at basketball, go to the part and shoot hoops in front of people.

Realize That Your Ego Will Never Go Away

Controlling and managing your ego will have to become a routine in your life. It will never fully go away and will rear its ugly head at the most inopportune times if you let your guard down. Always be on high alert of your ego trying to take over, and you will continue to overcome it.

You Are Not the Best

I am not trying to be insulting here, but knowing that you are not going to be the best in every situation means that you understand your limitations. Everyone has limitations, so there is no sense in feeling bad over them. Accept that you are not perfect, but recognize that it does mean you cannot accomplish your goals. You may just need to work harder and focus more on certain areas.

Imagine Your Ego as Another Person

This step may seem ridiculous, but imagine your ego as another person. It is best to picture someone that you may listen, but never actually take advice from, like a whining child. Now, once you imagine your ego in this manner, allow it to speak and say what it needs, acknowledge it with a "thank you," and then move on. When you can actually picture your ego in this way, it will do a lot in stopping you from making significant mistakes.

Stop Bragging

There is no need to brag about your accomplishments. If they are great enough, other people will do the talking for you. The less you talk about yourself, the more humble you become, and humility is a major aspect of self-esteem. You never feel the need to talk yourself up.

Be Grateful for the Little Things

Gratitude is great for improving your attitude. When you start being grateful for the little things, you do not worry so much about the big things. Also, remember that some people cannot have what you have, no matter how hard they try. With the same token, some people will be in a different position than you, that you are unable to reach. That is okay. Just focus on yourself and what you have.

Learn to Compliment Others

People with large egos have a hard time admitting when others have done a great job. They feel it will take the spotlight off of them. Practicing paying even the smallest compliments to other people can help you take the attention off of your ego problems.

On top of these practices, we have gone over, a few other ways to get rid of your ego include:

- Embrace a beginner's attitude. Try something new regularly that forces you to challenge yourself. This will help you realize that you are not perfect at everything.
- Concentrate on the effort you put in, and not the results. You will be forced to see how much you put into an activity, and determine if you did too much, or not enough.
- Never stop learning, even if it's not something you will ever use. It keeps you humble.
- Validate yourself once in a while.
- Never expect rewards or recognition. Do what is right, simply because it is the right thing to do.
- Do not try to control everything.

Forgiving People

Since so much of our self-esteem is tied up in what the people of our past did or did not do for us, it is important to forgive those who may have harmed us. We often hold onto grudges, and this prevents us from moving forward. Part of having self-esteem is no longer allowing others to control us. If the actions of people in the past still impact the opinion we have of ourselves, then we are still under there control. The main idea of forgiveness is that you have the ability to move on without having to carry a heavy burden any longer. Here is what forgiveness does not mean:

- Condoning harmful behavior.

- Accepting someone back into your life.

- Forgetting the incident or incidents that harmed you.

- Having to talk to the person again in any way.

- You are helping the other person. Of course, this may be a secondary benefit, which is fine.

By forgiving someone, you are accepting the reality that they did something terrible to you, but it no longer has to define you. Forgiveness is 100 percent for your own benefit.

The first step in forgiveness is the willingness to actually forgive someone. Just imagine that the anger you have for someone is a bag of rocks that you have been carrying on your back. After many years, this becomes very exhausting, both physically and mentally. Now, imagine that forgiveness means dropping that bag of rocks forever. You will feel much better when you put down the bag, and you will feel much better once you forgive. When you are ready, then utilize the following steps to help you get past, well, your past.

- Think about the particular incidents that angered you. Accept that they happened and what your feelings were when they did. In order to forgive, you must acknowledge what happened. You cannot just ignore it. This is why forgetting is not part of the process. For example, the incident could have been that your parents were absent and did not pay any attention to you.

- Acknowledge the growth in yourself that happened after the incident occurred. What did it make you learn about yourself and the world? For example, if your parents were absent for much of your life, perhaps it taught you how to be independent and survive on your own. That is a pretty big deal.

- Now think about the other person. The one that actually caused the incident. Realize that they were working from a limited frame of mind and did not have the benefit of hindsight. When they harmed you in some way, they were probably trying to have one of their needs met. Think about what that need may have been, and if it changes your perspective on them. In reference to your parents, maybe they were absent and did not pay attention to you because they were worried about always having food on the table and a roof over your head. This caused them to work incessantly, and when they were home, they were too tired to give you the right amount of attention. It's possible that they hated being absent just as much as you did.

- Finally, say the words, "I forgive you." It is up to you whether you want to tell the person or not. In any event, tell yourself.

Forgiveness will help you put closure on your past so that you can focus on moving forward. This is an important step forward to gaining self-esteem. You will no longer be bound by what happened to you in the past; therefore, you will be free.

Overcoming Trauma

Since trauma plays a major role in a person's self-image, it is important to identify the negative thoughts that will lead to low self-esteem. Once you catch these thoughts, then you can combat them head-on. You may never forget about the trauma, but just like the hurt you received from people of your past, you can keep it from controlling you. The following are a few simple steps you can take to help you improve your negative self-image related to trauma. These practices have been used widely with people suffering from Post Traumatic Stress Disorder.

- Identify your negative thoughts. Once negative thoughts become part of your routine, they can easily slip by without getting caught. Self-monitoring can be a great way of increasing awareness of your thoughts and how they are affecting your mood and behavior. You must do this consciously. You may also sit down at the end of each day and run down what you did. Think about all of the negative thoughts you had, what caused them, and how you reacted. This can also make you more aware of them in the future. We often have specific triggers that affect our mood.

- Once you learn to identify negative thoughts, slow them down. The more you think about negative thoughts, the more intense they become. Therefore, once you identify them, distract yourself by thinking of something else. This is not about avoidance, but taking a step back and reducing the intensity of these thoughts. Often times, we cannot deal with negativity because it becomes so overwhelming. Once we remove ourselves from the situation a little bit, then we can manage things more appropriately.

- After reducing the intensity of your thoughts, it is now time to challenge them. Many times, we accept our thoughts at face value without actually questioning them. As a result, we do not actually know why we are thinking negatively during a certain situation. We just know that we always have. Challenge your thoughts by asking some of the following questions:

    o What evidence is there for having these thoughts?
    o What evidence is there that are against these thoughts?
    o Are there moments when these thoughts have not been true?
    o Do I only have these thoughts when I am sad, angry, or depressed, or do I have them when I am feeling okay, as well?
    o What advice would I give someone else who is also having these thoughts?

o Is there any type of alternate explanation?

- Counter your negative thoughts further by using positive self-supportive statements. For example, you can tell yourself all of your recent accomplishments, the good qualities you do possess, or positive things you are looking forward to in the future, like starting a new job or taking a vacation. Basically, counter negative thoughts with positive ones. It is beneficial to write some of these down so you can refer to them in the future. When you are drowning in negativity, it can be difficult to come up with positive statements about yourself.

- As a side note, you do not have to use positive self-supportive statements exclusively when you are upset. You can tell them to yourself any time to build up your positivity.

Chapter 4: Changing Our Minds

For the final chapter in this section, we can start focusing on shifting the mindest fully towards high self-esteem. Once this occurs, we must continue to follow the strategies I have gone over to never lose your self-esteem. If you let your guard down, it will happen.

How To Ignore Things

Our self-esteem continues to remain low throughout our lives because we always let things bother us. Many of these things are beyond our control, so we should not pay them any mind. The reason people achieve their lifelong goals is that they don't let their surroundings affect their minds. The following are some ways to ignore what bothers you, so you can keep moving forward while loving yourself.

Stop Comparing Yourself To Others

The bottom line is, you are not someone else, and they are not you. Just because someone else looks great in a dress or suit, does not mean you have to, as well. Also, understand that other people will not look as good as you in certain outfits. Some people will look great all dressed up, while others pull off the casual look better.

If you are not comfortable, then you will never feel right in any situation. Therefore, do not force yourself into something, simply because other people are doing it. Understand yourself through self-awareness and focus on the things that make you feel good. You can't compare yourself to others, and they can't compare themselves to you. Work on impressing the person in the mirror and no one else.

Ignore Societal Pressure

Have you ever done something because someone you don't like or even know might become impressed, even though they don't actually care about you? If this statement sounds ridiculous, imagine actually living. Oh, wait! Many people are already. This is because they are under some sort of societal pressure to live a certain way, even though most people in society don't matter to them in the long run. To stop allowing this to happen, ask yourself the following questions.

- Who will be responsible after I kill my dreams to produce a fake image, society, or me?
- Are the people around me genuinely concerned about my happiness? If not, then why do I care so much?
- Will the people pressuring me even matter five years from now?
- Am I alone in feeling this societal pressure?

After answering all of these questions, you will realize that your situation is not unique. Many people are pressured by society and trying to hold up a fake image. This means they are not happy because they are not willing to share their true selves. Ultimately, you will be living your own existence, whether you choose it or someone else does.

Start Living In The Present Moment

So many people live in the past, and therefore, their old mistakes still have an impact on their present state of mind. It's time to get over your past. The following are some tips to help you do so.

- Create some physical distance between yourself and the person or situation that is reminding you of your past. This could mean cutting off some close people or physically moving somewhere else.

- Stay busy working and improving yourself, that you have no time to worry about what happened in the past.

- Treat yourself like you would a best friend. We tend to be gentler with others than ourselves.

- Don't shut out negative emotions. Let them flow through you so you can overcome them.

- Don't expect an apology from other people. Even if you were wronged by them, they might not think so. Therefore, move on and accept that they haven't come to terms with anything, but you have.

- Give yourself permission to talk about your pain, even if it's just to yourself. In any event, let it out. Let the past pain escape out of you.

Leverage Your Purpose

This will give your life more meaning. First, leverage your purpose to serve others. Help someone else realize their dreams through your own unique talents. There are many unique ways to do this, including teaching, coaching, and mentoring. Do this on a volunteer basis. Whatever gives purpose to your life, share it with someone else.

Try out these different practices and feel yourself start ignoring all of the noise around you. It is distracting, and you must be able to filter it.

The Mindset Shift

We have gone over many different aspects of the mind and how to change certain thought-processes. What happens with these techniques is a total mindset shift. Instead of your mind being wired to think negatively about everything, including yourself, you will now habitually think in a positive way and understand the values you bring to the world, which are a lot. The goal of all of the previous practices and strategies is to rewire your neural pathways to help change your mindset.

Your mindset was developed over a long period of time, which means the neural pathways you have are build up pretty strong. For this reason, they must be worked on regularly to help break them down and build new ones up. So, do not treat these techniques as a one-and-done cure. They must become a regular part of your lifestyle. Once they are, then you will be amazed at the results you have. When your self-esteem is high, you will:

- Have no problem being yourself.

- Be able to disagree without attacking someone.

- Not be swayed so easily by the opinions of others.

- Be able to articulate your views and be able to defend them appropriately when challenged.

- No longer fear uncertainty.

- Be much more resilient and tough.

- Never need approval from anyone to live your life as you choose.

- Value yourself and have high self-worth, despite what others may think of you.

- Not act like you know everything.

- Be okay with not being perfect.

- Never again let your past define who you are.

Once you go from low to high self-esteem, you will feel like a completely different person. You will still acknowledge your past pain, but it will not control you.

Now That Your Self-Esteem is High

After going through all of the practices, thoughts, and feelings inside of you will be different because you will have effectively restructured your mind. The plan now is to keep revisiting these techniques, so you never fall back into the abyss ever again. Now that your self-esteem is high, you will sense the following beliefs flowing through you.

- No matter what you've done, you are worthy of love. You understand your past mistakes, but will not degrade yourself over them.

- You are not defined by your "stuff." You will enjoy what you have, but your happiness will not be dependent on it.

- You will allow yourself to feel all of your emotions, and not be ashamed of them.

- You won't care if you miss out on things. You will feel okay about staying alone because your company is good enough.

- You will not be worried about what happens to you, because you will be able to respond appropriately, There will be challenges, but the end result will be in your favor.

- You will be doing what you love. You will look forward to every day.

- You will understand that people are judging you based on something within themselves.

- You will never think the world revolves around you. There is a higher power out there greater than anything that exists on Earth. This does not have to be a diety, but it certainly can be for you.

- You will find things to be grateful for every day. Because you are looking, you will find them.

PART II

Chapter 1: Self-Confidence In Various Situations

"Each time we face our fear, we gain strength, courage, and confidence in the doing."

-Theodore Roosevelt

While we have been speaking of self-worth and self-value, the focus of this chapter will be self-confidence, which is a different subject altogether.

Self-confidence is when you have faith in yourself and your abilities in a particular situation, and it does not relate to overall self-worth. If your self-confidence levels are low, it is because you are not comfortable in a particular setting, for whatever reason.

To help make self-confidence more clear, here are a few scenarios that showcase it in different circumstances.

- A doctor is self-confident when he performs any type of procedure within his specialty. He has so much training and experience that he truly believes in his skills and abilities to perform in various situations at work. When this same doctor goes for a hike, he does not have the same level of confidence in conquering a high peak, because he is out of shape.

- A mechanic can fix any car with his eyes closed. He has been a mechanic for so many years, that he is confident there is nothing that will come into his garage that he cannot handle. When this mechanic tries to work on the plumbing in his home, he is not very successful and has no confidence in his ability to perform the tasks.

- A great artist is confident in his ability to paint a portrait. If you ask him to solve a math problem, he has no confidence whatsoever.

These examples showcase how self-confidence can truly be based on the state of affairs, depending on what a person is facing at the moment. To handle a situation well, you must have self-confidence in your ability to do so. Self-confidence is gained through training, education, repetition, and life experience. It is impossible to be confident in every situation you ever come across, but the more you are willing to learn, the more confidence you will gain throughout life.

How a Lack of Self-Confidence Affects Us

As I mentioned before, self-confidence is circumstantial and will impact various areas of your life differently. Depending on how much experience, knowledge, or training, we have in different aspects of life, our confidence will ebb and flow. The key is to have self-confidence in the important areas of our lives, where it really matters. There are many examples in our everyday lives where self-confidence will play a major role.

Regarding the work setting, people who lack confidence in this arena cannot perform their necessary duties at an adequate level. This means poor job performance, being overlooked for raises and promotions, and even being let go from a position. If a person performs their job well, low self-confidence can still impact their desire to move up the latter. If they are confident in their particular position but do not feel confident at a higher level, like management, then they won't go after the promotion. They will simply stay put, even though they have the potential to do more.

Concerning starting a business, a certain level of confidence is needed to perform numerous tasks. There are many independent skills involved in running a business, and chances are, you will be doing most of them yourself when you first start. You need to have the proper training and education in these different areas, like finance, setting a budget, and marketing, etc., or you will not succeed in them. If you feel you can't do them yourself, then you may have to higher someone to do so. It may be worth it to avoid errors.

Self-confidence matters in our personal lives too. In order to find friends or develop relationships, we must have confidence in our abilities to form them. For example, it takes a lot of confidence for a man to walk up to a woman and say, "hi." To make friends, you must have the courage to talk to people. To learn new things and experience a new adventure, you must also have confidence in yourself to perform them. Once again, confidence comes from experience, and the more you put yourself out there, the more confident you will become.

Confidence is crucial in specific social settings. For example, during a work meeting, a lack of confidence can hold you back from speaking up, even if you have something very important to say. You won't get the necessary information out there that many people in the meeting could receive value from. This also relates to socializing with friends. You may have a friend who is harming themselves, but because you are uncertain how they will react, you ca nothing. You do not have the confidence that you will be able to respond appropriately.

A lack of confidence does not allow you to communicate assertively, which is important in order to get what you want. Instead of asking for things directly, you will beat around the bush and hope that the person will pick up on your clues. You will also use minimizing language, like "Sort of" or "kind of." This type of communication makes it seem like you lack conviction, and no one will take you seriously. You will just appear weak. Being assertive is essential, whether you are asking for something at working or setting boundaries with your friends.

If you suffer from low self-confidence, then every aspect of your life will suffer. We will get into different ways of increasing your confidence in the next chapter. For now, we will discuss how self-confidence works in different settings, especially in those that create anxiety for everybody.

Chapter 2: Social Anxiety

For this chapter, I will provide more detail for a specific type of confidence issue, and that is social anxiety.

Social Anxiety and Lack of Confidence In Specific Situations

Social anxiety is an actual disorder where a person has a phobia in which a person feels like they are being watched and judged by everybody. There may be select situations where this is actually happening, but in most circumstances, it is an unfound fear. This is an extreme situation where a person has a lack of confidence in everything they do, and therefore, feel like they are the center of attention.

Going for a job interview, taking a test, going on a date, or speaking in public are normal things that create anxiety in almost everybody. It is amplified greatly in someone who has a social anxiety disorder. Furthermore, these individuals actually become nervous during normal, everyday activities like shopping for food, parking their car, or using a public restroom. Their anxiety is so intense that they feel judged in every moment of their lives. This fear can become so strong that it interferes with people going to work, attending school, talking to their friends, or doing any other menial task during the day.

It is estimated that about seven percent of the American population suffers from social anxiety. While this number is not massive, it shows that the problem is not uncommon.

Researchers believe there is a genetic component where areas of the brain that deal with fear and anxiety are involved. However, there is no explanation as to why some family members are affected while others are not. For example, out of two siblings, one may be shy and quiet, while the other one is loud and bombastic.

Another cause of social anxiety may be underdeveloped social skills. Some individuals will feel discouraged after talking to people, even if the conversation did not go poorly, which will cause them to avoid interactions in the future. The lack of interaction will just lead to further underdeveloped social skills, and the social anxiety trend will continue.

Many people with this disorder do not have anxiety in specific social settings, but instead in areas where performance is involved. This is often referred to as performance anxiety and is related to performing in front of a crowd in any type of capacity, whether it is a speech, dance recital, or sporting event. Speaking in public is one of the worst fears that people have, and in some surveys, it is number one. Jerry Seinfeld used to make the joke that during a funeral, most people would rather be inside the casket than the ones giving the eulogy.

Even if a person is confident in the subject matter, having to discuss it in a large crowd, with hundreds, or even thousands, of eyes, looking at them, will create a high level of anxiety. This situation would be unsettling for many people. There are many reasons why someone would have a fear of speaking in public, and it goes beyond just being nervous.

Fear and anxiety will create a physiological response within us. During this process, our autonomic nervous system, which works as a protective mechanism by keeping us alert, will make us hyper-arousable. Generally, this is done to put the body in a state of battle. As a result, we will have an emotional experience to fear, which will interfere with our ability to perform well in front of an audience.

Another factor to consider is the person's beliefs about the speaking engagement. Many people will feel that if they screw up something in front of a crowd, it will hurt their credibility, and therefore, their careers. They also feel that their performance will never be forgotten, and their whole public image will be destroyed in an instant. The fact that everyone has a camera on their phones lends some more credibility to this fear. These feelings cause people to overthink and become extremely anxious beyond their control.

Anxiety during a public speech is greater in those who don't do it often. The more a person speaks in front of a crowd, the less nervous they become over time. Unfortunately, most people do not speak in front of audiences constantly, unless they do it for a living. If someone only speaks a few times a year or less, then they will usually have anxiety every time. Also, a person's status in relation to the audience members can play a role in their confidence levels. For example, if a person is speaking in front of high-level executives about a topic they already know, then this can create an immense amount of fear. They worry about having their speech dissected. What a person must realize here is that it is not so much the content of the speech, but how it is presented.

The most obvious reason for the fear of public speaking is the actual skill involved. Speaking in front of an audience involves getting the people engaged.

This is done by proper timing, eye contact, stage presences, charisma, and a little bit of humor. The bottom line is, you must be able to connect with the audience somehow, or they will not care whatsoever what you have to say, no matter who you are. Your status may capture their attention for a while, but if you can't keep their attention, your speech will be forgotten before it even starts. Many people know this and are worried that they won't be able to hold their audience's attention.

The more anxious you are, the less likely you are to perform well. It is to your advantage to be as relaxed as possible and overcome your social anxiety, which is much easier said than done.

Aside from public speaking, another social situation that can cause anxiety is being in a large crowd. Many people with social anxiety are okay when they are just around their friends. However, once the circle starts increasing, their anxiety grows tremendously. This type of fear is known as enochlophobia, and it is related to the perceived dangers posed by large gatherings of people you may see in everyday life. The fear includes getting lost, stuck, or harmed in some manner by the crowd.

Most of you are probably thinking of concerts or other places where organized gatherings occur. The simple solution here would be to avoid these types of events. However, this fear also encompasses busy metropolitan areas, public transits like the bus or subway, or even workspaces with a lot of employees. Any type of space where a large number of people are, a person with this type of phobia will become fearful and anxious.

In the next chapter, we will describe various ways to build up your self-confidence, so you can be prepared to handle any situation, even if you are not familiar with it.

Chapter 3: Learning to Become Comfortable

When you lack self-confidence, it means you are unsure of yourself in a particular setting. You have a certain level of discomfort, which precludes you from going all-in when performing a certain task. Unfortunately, if your confidence levels are not high enough, then you will not perform at your highest level. This does not mean you aren't nervous or slightly anxious. It literally means that you do not believe in yourself in a specific situation.

A person will never feel fully confident in every aspect of life. There will be plenty of times when we are faced with something new, and it will completely throw us off our game. The goal of this chapter will be to build self-esteem in some of the most important areas of our lives and also develop the critical thinking skills we need to overcome almost any situation, no matter how unfamiliar it may be.

Building Your Self-Confidence

Nobody is born with an unlimited amount of self-confidence. Also, people are not born with zero confidence. It is something that either gets built-up or deteriorated over time. Unfortunately, many people have had their confidence shattered so many times that they never have confidence in themselves in any situation, no matter how familiar they are with it. The practices in this section will focus on building self-confidence in the general sense, so you are ready to attack life, no matter what gets thrown your way.

Groom Yourself Regularly

This may sound obvious, but many people do not realize how good they will feel when they take the time to shower, do their hair, clean their nails, and dress nicely. The old saying, "When you look good, you feel good," Holds a lot of truth. Even if you have nothing important planned for the day, take the time to groom yourself. You will automatically feel more confident in any situation you come across. You don't have to go to the salon every day or wear thousand-dollar suits. The goal is to look good when you observe yourself in the mirror. This could mean wearing your favorite shirt and jeans combination.

Photoshop Your Self-Image

We take a lot of stock in our self-image. No matter how much we try to say that looks don't matter, we like to look at ourselves in the mirror and see a positive self-image. You can alter your self-image by mentally photoshopping yourself in a way that is positive to you. You can then work on obtaining this image in real-life. For example, if you see yourself 20 pounds lighter, then keep this image in your mind and work towards it.

Destroy Negative Thoughts

No matter how unfamiliar you are with a situation, you are more likely to handle it well if you get rid of your negative thoughts. These simply take up space in your mind and have no value in your productivity. Be aware of our self-talk and how you think about yourself. This may sound ridiculous, but when you find a negative thought entering your mind, picture it as an object or creature that you want to destroy. For example, when you begin having negative thoughts, picture them as bugs. Now, squash those bugs mentally, and you will effectively destroy your negative thoughts. This is a great mental trick to play on yourself. After getting rid of the negative thought, replace it with a positive one.

Get to Know Yourself

When going into battle, it is best to know your enemy very well, no matter who they are. When you are dealing with low self-confidence, your enemy becomes yourself. This is why it is important to get to know yourself as well as you can. Listen intently to your thoughts, write about yourself in a journal, determine what thoughts about yourself dominate your mind, and analyze why you have negative thoughts.

Next, write down all of the positive aspects that you have, no matter how minuscule they may seem. Start thinking about the limitations you have and determine if they are real and verified, or just something you came up with in your head. Dig as deep you can get into your psyche, and you will find out more about yourself than you had ever known. The more you know about yourself, the greater self-confidence you will have.

Be Kind and Generous

Be kind and generous to others, whether it is time, money, or other resources, will be great for improving your self-image. When you are genuinely able to help someone when they need you, then it makes you feel good about who you are. It gives you a sense of purpose.

Be Prepared

Be as prepared for life as you can. Think about this for a moment: if you are taking an exam, and have not studied, then you won't be prepared, and your confidence level will be very low. On the other hand, if you did study intensely, then you will be much more prepared and have a greater amount of confidence. Imagine life as one big exam. The more prepared you are every day, the more confident you will feel in any situation. The following are some general ways you can be more prepared.

- Have plenty of food in the refrigerator and cabinets.
- Have a substantial emergency fund.
- Have the basics as far as emergency supplies at all times.
- If you have something specific planned for that day, like a presentation or meeting, be as prepared as possible for it.
- Always be on alert for dangerous situations.

Know Your Principles and Live By Them

What are the main principles upon which your life is built? If you are not sure, then it's time to sit down and really think about it. Otherwise, your life will be completely directionless. When you know your principles and live by them, then you are truly living your passion, and this is great for your self-confidence. People who are simply coasting through life with no real values will have no goals in life either. They are simply existing and not fully living. When you refuse to live your life based on your values, then you lack confidence in yourself.

Speak Slowly

Speaking slowly will make a huge difference in how people perceive you. It shows a sense of knowledge and confidence in what is being said. Someone who speaks with a rapid-fire approach generally does so because they are not confident in what they are saying. They just want to get the word out there and hope nobody calls them out. Even if you don't feel totally confident on a subject, try speaking slowly anyway, and see how much your self-confidence actually builds. This can be a great mind trick. When you speak slow, you have more time to formulate good thoughts. Of course, I am not telling you to take it to the extreme here, just don't spit words out like a machine gun.

Stand Up Straight

This is another simple trick to help you feel better about yourself. When you slouch, not only does it showcase a lack of confidence, you actually have less self-confidence. This goes along the lines of looking good and feeling good. And trust me, when you stand up straighter, you will look much better.

Increase Your Competence Levels

Simply put, if you are more competent in something, you feel more confident. You gain competence through practice and training. In any situation in life, get as much training as you can to feel as fully self-confident as you can. Let's use the example of a house fire. I hope that your house never burns down, but if it does, I want you to feel confident that you and your family can escape safely. Map out an escape plan and practice it as often as you can. Many companies do quarterly evacuation drills. Employ this same practice in your house. If an emergency like this ever occurs, you will have more competence, and therefore, confidence in being able to handle it. Think of as many possible circumstances as you can in life, and determine ways to practice and train in them.

Set Small Goals and Achieve Them

When you are able to achieve a goal in life, it is a huge boost to your confidence. Set small goals regularly and then work hard to accomplish them. Remember, they should be small and reasonable. You can even cut down larger goals into smaller achievable steps. For example, if your goal is to buy a car, you can create a goal to save a certain amount of money by the end of the month, and then every month after that.

Change Small Habits About Yourself

Trying to change a large habit all at once can be very difficult, and the chances of failure are high. This will be a huge shot to your confidence. Instead, focus on smaller habits that will lead to big change. For example, if your goal is to wake up early and workout before starting your day, then don't try to wake up two hours earlier on the first day. Start by waking up 10-20 minutes early until it becomes a habit, and then increase the time from there as you feel comfortable.

Focus Your Attention on Solutions

So often, we are completely focused on the problems and pay no attention to the solutions. For example, you may always complain about being tired, but do nothing to change it, because the solutions never enter your mind. Make it a habit to focus on solutions whenever a problem enters your mind. You will get more accomplished and gain a lot of self-confidence. For example, if you are tired every day, then what is making you that way. Are you not sleeping enough? If not, then why is that? Are you eating too much sugar before going to bed? Do you have a poor diet during the day? Are you drinking enough water? See how man questions you can get answered if you just shift your focus from the problems to the solutions. Try it out with any small problems that you may have and notice the results.

Become Active

You may have noticed that when you start taking action, work starts getting done. So often, people sit around and worry about how they will get something done, rather than doing the work to get it done. Excessive worry leads to a lack of confidence. The more you worry, the lower your self-confidence will become. If you take action, you will obtain results. Results lead to increased confidence. Next time you find yourself worrying about something, start developing a plan and execute it. Hours of taking actions will give you better results than hours of sitting around and worrying.

Gain More Knowledge

Empowering yourself with knowledge is one of the greatest ways to build self-confidence. You will never know everything, but the more you know, the better you will feel about yourself. This goes along the same vein as building competence. You become more knowledgeable on a subject by studying and practicing it. This does not have to be something you will use. It can just be for your own self-fulfillment. According to psychology, one of the biggest reasons for low self-confidence is either misinformation or a lack of information. As you become more empowered with knowledge, you will gain more information too.

Just like with the steps to gain self-esteem, these previous steps must be employed regularly. Our self-confidence will be challenged all the time, so it is in our best interest to build it up regularly through practice and discipline. Think of your confidence as a muscle that you must work out every single day. Do this, and you will be amazed at how much self-confidence you have throughout your life.

Overcoming Procrastination

People love to procrastinate. And why wouldn't they? Why do something now if you can do it tomorrow? I'll tell you why. What keeps you from making the same excuse tomorrow? Also, how do you know what tomorrow will bring? Perhaps something will happen that prevents you from doing the task then, too. A better question to ask yourself is: Why wait until tomorrow if you can get it done now.

Procrastination is a huge problem in our society, and it leads to a lot of anxiety. This anxiety, in turn, leads to a lack of self-confidence. Procrastination is basically a form of being unprepared. Let's say you have a project due on Friday, and it is now Monday. If you begin working on it now, and do a little bit each day, you will have more confidence in completing the project and doing it well, than you would if you started on Thursday. Imagine how much more thorough you can be by starting projects a little bit earlier. The following are a few easy action steps you can take to help overcome procrastination.

- Do not take on more than you can handle. Keep the number of decisions you have to make to a minimum. The more you have to decide on, the more likely you are to procrastinate.

- Begin focusing on the benefits of completing something, rather than the task. For example, if you are working on a project for work, imagine how good it will feel when it's done. Also, think about the rewards that might come if you perform the task well, like a promotion or raise. This focus on the benefits will give you more motivation to get started.

- Prepare yourself for a task by becoming educated on it. Be aware of your limitations before even picking up a new project and do what you can to obtain the necessary knowledge before moving forward. Once again, knowledge will lead to confidence, and confidence makes you active in a pursuit.

- Turn distractions into rewards. If you cannot get your work done because you are always binge-watching shows, then force yourself to turn them into rewards after a hard day's work. For example, set a timer for three hours and use that time to focus on your projects. After the three hours, pat yourself on the back and watch an episode of the show you like. Remember that you have to stay disciplined.

- Set up a daily schedule system for yourself. For example, the first two hours in the morning are designated for the most important tasks, then a break, followed by two hours of the less important tasks, then another break, and finally, dedicating the last part of the day towards the least important tasks. Once you set up a schedule, stick to it to the best of your ability.
- Avoid getting stuck on a project. Give yourself a certain amount of time on a specific task, and if you cannot make progress, move onto something else and revisit it later. There is no sense in wasting time being nonproductive on something.

Follow these steps religiously and watch procrastination be an afterthought in your life.

Build Confidence At Work

Our jobs are a major part of our lives, and it is important to have self-confidence in this environment. We went over building self-confidence in the general sense earlier in this chapter, and now we will focus on more specific areas in our lives. Many of the action steps and techniques are still the same, while some will be more geared towards work.

- Cut out the negative self-talk. Do not beat yourself up at work. It will do nothing for you. Speaking kindly and encouragingly to yourself and you will learn from whatever mistakes you made more easily.

- Boost your knowledge any way you can, and it is a surefire way to achieve confidence. Stay up on the latest research, services, and products within your company and industry as a whole. Imagine being able to bring an idea to your workplace simply because you read up on it. This will make you feel very good about yourself. Always try to stay ahead of the curve.

- Use opportunities to teach others who know less about a subject than you do. Being able to teach others effectively will boot your own knowledge and confidence.

- Practice what you know incessantly, and always look for ways to improve. Identify and correct mistakes along the way.

- Do not speak poorly about others. This already shows a lack of confidence in yourself. When you compliment and speak highly of other people, you acknowledge their strengths and make them feel good about themselves. In turn, you feel good about yourself, too. This also helps to build a nontoxic work environment.

- Pick up new skills to enhance proficiency at your job.

- Ask questions when you do not know something. You may think that you will feel stupid if you ask a question. However, asking and then doing it right, is a bigger boost to confidence than not asking and screwing things up.

- Eliminate negative language, even if it's not geared at anybody. Negative language can affect our psyche on the deepest levels, effectively lowering our confidence levels without us even realizing it.

- Focus on all of the success you have had at work, rather than the failures.

Chapter 4: Getting Rid of Social Anxiety

Social anxiety encompasses many areas of our lives, such as personal relationships, engaging in activities, hanging out in large groups, or giving public speeches. In order to engage in any of these areas, we must overcome our social anxiety, which is essentially having a lack of confidence in social settings. Depending on the individual, social anxiety will either impact them no matter what setting they're, while for others, it will be more selective. For example, a person may be very talkative and confident among his friends but will be terrified when speaking or performing on stage.

This can be the other way around, too. Legendary late-night host, Johnny Carson, was magnanimous on stage but known to be quiet, reserved, and even shy in small groups. We will go over some basic techniques to improve your social anxiety. These will be effective in just about any setting you are in. These techniques are involved with cognitive behavioral therapy, which is a psychologically-based approach to dealing with anxiety, that is drugfree.

- Think about what you're avoiding. As always, the first step in solving a problem is by identifying what it is. What specific social settings are you avoiding. For instance, some people have stated things like using a public restroom, ordering food at a restaurant, becoming scared in a large group, or speaking up at a meeting. Determine what settings cause your social anxiety. Write these down somewhere so you can keep track.

- Now, take your list that you made and develop some type of rating system. This is used to determine the level of anxiety you might experience in each situation to determine what makes it worse. If you feel the most anxious while giving a public speech, then you can rate that as a 10, and then move down from there. So if being around friends gives you none or very little anxiety, that can be a 0 or 1 rating. These ratings are based mainly on predictions. Basically, we are predicting how we would react in certain social settings.

- The next step is to test your predictions. Go out and put yourself in specific situations that may or may not give you the level of anxiety you predicted. For instance, you may have thought you would be at a level of 9 when meeting someone new at a party, but once you did, it was actually around a 4 rating. You may surprise yourself at how well you can actually cope with your anxiety.

- Identify safety behaviors that you use and work to eliminate them. These are superstitious behaviors that people engage in to make them feel safer. I am not talking about carrying a rabbit's foot. Safety behaviors are things like pre-medicating before a social event, avoiding eye contact, rehearsing what you're going to say, or walking with stiff shoulders. The main problem with these types of behaviors is that you will believe they are the only way to get through an anxiety-casing situation. The more you give up these behaviors, the better your experience will be. Imagine how much better a conversation will be when it's natural, rather than scripted.

- Challenge your anxious thoughts. Instead of thinking about how bad things will go, start thinking about how they will go well. If you are worried about looking foolish, ask yourself why that is, and when have you actually looked foolish in the past? Is it real or made up in your head.

- Practice doing what makes you anxious. The classic example here is giving a speech in front of a mirror or recording yourself while you speak alone in your living room. Remind yourself that people don't usually know what your internal feelings are unless you make it obvious to them. This means that no one may have noticed your anxiety in the past. Eventually, test out what you've practiced in the real world. In the case of a speech, after practicing alone for a while, you can perform it in front of some friends.

- Practice self-reward, rather than post-mortem. Post-mortem means that a person analyzes and criticizes every little thing that they've done during a social encounter. If they were standing awkwardly, they become focused on that. Instead, reward yourself for facing the anxiety-causing situation.

Remember to always rinse and repeat with all of these techniques. They must be done regularly until you develop a pattern. You will never be fully confident in every situation. The world will throw things at you that will make you take a few steps back and throw you off your game. That is okay. The key to these exercises is to build up a certain level of self-confidence so that you will be ready to engage and deal with whatever life throws at you. You will develop true strength and knowledge to overcome, no matter how unfamiliar a situation is.

PART III

Chapter 1: Self-Care Is the Best Care

"It is so important to take time for yourself and find clarity. The most important relationship is the one you have with yourself."

-Diane Von Furstenberg

Self-care is any activity that we deliberately do to improve our own well-being, whether it is physical, emotional, mental, or spiritual. The importance of taking care of one's self cannot be denied, as even health care training focuses on making sure healthcare workers are caring for themselves. If you do not take care of yourself, eventually, every other aspect o your life will fall apart, including your ability to help others.

This is a very simple concept, yet it is highly overlooked in the grand scheme of things. People lack the tendency to look after themselves and put their needs before anyone else. Good self-care is essential to improving our mood and reducing our anxiety levels. It will do wonders for reducing exhaustion and burnout, which is very common in our fast-paced world. It will also lead to positive improvements in our relationships.

One thing to note is that self-care does not mean forcing ourselves to do something we don't like, no matter how enjoyable it is to other people. For example, if your friends are forcing you to go to a party you rather not attend, then giving in is not taking care of yourself. If you would rather stay in and watch a movie, then that's what you should do, and it will be better for your well-being.

How Does Self-Care Work

It is difficult to pinpoint exactly what self-care is, as it is personal for everybody. Some people love to pamper themselves by going to the spa, while others enjoy physical activities like hiking, biking, or swimming. Some individuals take up art or other hobbies, like writing or playing a musical instrument. These activities are all different but will have the same type of benefits for the individuals engaging in them.

The main factor to consider when engaging in self-care is to determine if you enjoy the activity in question. If not, then it's time to move on. Self-care is an active choice that you actually have to plan out. It is time you set aside for yourself to make sure all of your needs are met. If you use a planner of any sort, make sure to dedicate some space for your particular self-care activities. Also, let people who need to know about your plans so you can become more committed. Pay special attention to how you feel afterward. The objective of any self-care activity is to make yourself feel better. If this is not happening, then it's time to change the activity.

While self-care, as a whole, is individualized, there is a basic checklist to consider.

- Create a list of things you absolutely don't want to do during the self-care process. For instance, not checking emails, not answering the phone, avoiding activities you don't enjoy, or not going to specific gatherings, like a house party.
- Eat nutritious and healthy meals most of the time, while indulging once in a while.
- Get the proper amount of sleep according to your needs.
- Avoid too many negative things, like news or social media.
- Exercise regularly.
- Spend appropriate time with your loved ones. These are the people you genuinely enjoy and not forced relationships.
- Look for opportunities to enjoy yourself and laugh.
- Do at least one relaxing activity a day, like taking a bath, going for a walk, or cooking a meal.

Self-care is extremely important and should not be an anomaly in your life.

How Does Self-Care Improve Self-Esteem and Self-Confidence?

To bring everything full circle, self-care plays a major role in improving self-esteem and self-confidence. It is easy to see how taking care of yourself will also make you feel better about yourself overall. All of these are actually inter-related, and a lack of one showcases a lack of the other. While caring for yourself also improves your self-esteem and self-confidence, not having self-esteem or self-confidence also leads to a lack of self-care. Basically, you believe that you are not good enough to be taken care of.

People with high self-esteem and self-confidence value themselves as much as they value others, and have no issues with making sure they're taken care of. They realize that it does not make them selfish or inconsiderate to think in this manner. Even if other people try to make them feel that way, a self-confident person will just brush off the criticism. An important thing to note is that when you take care of yourself, it does not mean you don't care about other people. It simply means you have enough self-love to not place yourself on the backburner.

Many people work so hard to try and please everyone else. This is one of the telltale signs of low self-esteem. While they're busy worried about other peoples' needs, their own get neglected, which will wear them down over time. The more they're unable to please someone, the harder they will try. What people in this situation don't realize is that some people are impossible to please, and it is not their responsibility to please them. That is up to the individual.

Poor self-care will eventually lead to poor self-image. It is possible that a person already has this initially. Self-care includes taking care of your hygienic and grooming needs. If you don't take the time to make yourself look good, this will significantly impact the value you place on yourself. When you are t work, among your friends, or just walking around town, not feeling like you look good will ultimately make you feel like you don't belong anywhere. Your confidence levels will plummet due to this.

Your health is another aspect to consider. Poor self-care means bad sleeping habits, unhealthy diets, lack of exercise, and more self-destructive behaviors. Your poor health practices can result in chronic illnesses down the line, like heart disease or diabetes. Once again, diminished health will lead to reduced self-confidence and self-esteem. Ask yourself now if putting other people ahead of you is worth it? I've got some news for you. The people who demand the most from you are probably looking out for themselves first.

The less a person takes care of themselves, the more their self-esteem and self-confidence will decline. It turns into a vicious downward cycle. This is why it is important to focus on all of these areas equally. When you find yourself neglecting your own self-care practices, it is time to shift your direction and bring your attention back to your needs. Ignoring your needs will ultimately lead to your fall. We will discuss specific practices and techniques for improving self-care in the next chapter.

Chapter 2: What Does Good Self-Care Look Like?

Good Self-Care Practices

The following are some ways that good self-care will look like. If you find
yourself having these qualities, then you are on the right path.

Taking Responsibility for Your Happiness

When you engage in self-care, it is truly self-care. This means you only rely on
yourself, and nobody else, to make sure your needs are met. You realize that
your happiness is no one else's responsibility but your own. You alone have the
ability to control your outcomes. As a result of this independence, you will
develop the skills and attitude you need to care for your own physical, mental,
emotional, and spiritual well-being.

You Become Assertive With Others

People often take assertiveness for rudeness. This is not true, but if people
believe that standing firm for what you want is rude, then that's their problem.
Once you reach a certain mindset where self-care is important to you, then you
will be unapologetically assertive. This means you have the ability to say "no"
with confidence and stand by it. "No" is a complete sentence, and people will
realize that quickly when they hear it from you.

You Treat Yourself As You Would a Close Friend

It's interesting how we believe that other people deserve better treatment from
us than we do ourselves. We have a tendency to put our best friends in front of
us, no matter how detrimental it is to our lives. This behavior stops once we
engage in proper self-care. At this point, you will treat yourself as good as, or
even better, than you treat your most beloved friends.

You Are Not Afraid to Ask for What You Want

Once you learn to take care of yourself, you also see your value increase within your mind. This means having an understanding that your voice, opinion, and needs matter, just like anybody with high self-esteem and self-confidence, would. As a result, you will not be afraid to ask for what you want, even if you might not get it.

Your Life Is Set Around Your Own Values

Once you practice self-care, you learn to check in with yourself before making important decisions. You always make sure the choices you are about to make line up with your purpose and values. If they go against them, then it's not a path you choose. This goes for the career you choose, where you decide to live, and the relationships you maintain in your life.

While all of the traits are focused on self, but it will lead to better relationships with other people too. When you practice self-care, you are in a better state in every aspect of your being. This gives you the ability to take care of and help those you need you, as well. Self-care is not an option, but a necessity, and it must never be ignored. Taking care of yourself is not selfish, no matter what anybody tells you. If someone tries to make you feel guilty over this matter, then consider distancing or removing them from your life. You are not obligated to maintain relationships with people.

Chapter 3: Demanding Your Own Self-Care

We went over the importance of self-care, and now we will focus on making it a reality in your life. If you want self-care to occur, you must be willing to demand it. The world is full of people who expect you to be at there beck-and-call every moment of the day. Some of these individuals are those who are closest to us, like friends or family members. This can make it harder to make our demands heard, but there is no way around it. Taking care of yourself is not an idea you can budge on. It is extremely important. We will go over several ways to maintain your ability for self-care in your life and provide detailed action steps to help you progress in this area.

Setting Healthy Boundaries

One of the biggest obstacles to self-care is other people who surround you. These are the true selfish individuals, whether they realize it or not, who believe they can barge in on your life and deserve all of your attention. They will take advantage of you, and if you are not careful, they will completely gain control of your emotions, and even your life. For proper self-care to occur, you must set firm and healthy boundaries with people. The following are steps that need to become mainstays in your life.

Identify and Name Your Limits

You must understand what your emotional, physical, mental, and spiritual limits are. If you do not know, then you will never be able to set real boundaries with people. Determine what behaviors you can tolerate and accept, and then consider what makes you feel uncomfortable. Identifying and separating these traits will help us determine our lines.

Stay Tuned Into Your Feelings

Two major emotions that are red flags that indicate a person is crossing a barrier are resentment or discomfort. Whenever you are having these feelings, it is important to determine why. Resentment generally comes from people taking advantage of us or feelings of being unappreciated. In this instance, we are likely pushing ourselves beyond our limits because we feel guilty. Guilt-trips is a weapon that many people use to get their way. It is important to recognize when someone is trying to make you feel guilty because they are way overstepping their boundaries. Resentment could also be due to someone imposing their own views or values onto us. When someone makes you feel uncomfortable, that is another indication of a boundary crossed. Stay in tune with both of these emotions.

Don't Be Afraid of Being Direct

With some people, setting boundaries is easy because they have a similar communication style. They can simply read your cues and back off when needed. For other individuals, a more direct approach is needed. Some people just don't get the hint that they've crossed a line. You must communicate to them in a firm way that they have crossed your limits, and you need some space. A respectful person will honor your wishes without hesitation. If they don't, then that's on them. Your personal space is more important than their feelings.

Give Yourself Permission to Set Boundaries

The potential downfalls to personal limits are fear, self-doubt, and guilt. We may fear the other person's response when we set strong boundaries. Also, we may feel guilty if they become emotional about it. We may even have self-doubt on whether we can maintain these limits in the long run. Many individuals have the mindset that in order to be a good daughter, son, parent, or friend, etc., we have to say "yes" all the time. They often wonder if they deserve to have boundaries and limits with those closest to them. The answer is, yes, you do. You need to give yourself permission to set limits with people because they are essential to maintaining healthy relationships too. Boundaries are also a sign of self-respect. Never feel bad for respecting yourself.

Consider Your Past and Present

Determine what roles you have played throughout your life in the various relationships you have had. Were you the one who was always the caretaker? If so, then your natural tendency may be to put others before yourself. Also, think about your relationships now. Are you the one always taking care of things, or is it a reciprocal relationship? For example, are you always the one making plans, buying gifts, having dinner parties, and being responsible for all of the important aspects of the relationships? If this is the case, then tuning into your needs is especially important here. If you are okay with the dynamics of the relationship, then that's fine. I can't tell you how to feel. However, if you feel anger and resentment over this, then it's time to let your feeling be known, unapologetically.

Be Assertive

Once again, this does not mean being rude, even though some people will interpret it that way. Being assertive simply means being firm, which is important when reminding someone about your boundaries. Creating boundaries alone is not enough. You also have to stand by them and let people know immediately if they've crossed them. Let the person know in a respectful but strong tone that you are uncomfortable with where they're going, and they need to give you some space. Assertive communication is a necessity.

Start Small

Setting boundaries is a skill that takes a while to develop, especially if it's something you've never done before. Therefore, start with a small boundary, like no phone calls after a certain time at night. Make sure to follow through; otherwise, the boundary is worthless. From here, make larger boundaries based on your comfort level.

Eliminating Toxicity and Not Caring About Losing Friends

If you plan on making self-care a priority in your life, I think that's great, and so should you. However, some people will have a problem with this. People don't always like it when their friends, family members, or acquaintances, etc., put themselves at the forefront of their lives. Once again, that is their problem, not yours. What is your problem, though, is distancing or even eliminating these individuals from your life. We will go over that in this section because part of self-care is eliminating toxicity from your life and not feeling bad about it.

Don't Expect People to Change

While everyone deserves a chance to redeem themselves, there comes the point where we must accept that people cannot change by force. They have to find it within themselves to make this change, and it is not our responsibility to do so. You may yearn to be the one who changes them, but it's usually a hopeless project. Toxic individuals are motivated by their problems. They use them to get the attention they need. Stop being the one to give it to them.

Establish and Maintain Boundaries

I already went in-depth on this, so I won't revisit it too much here. Just know that toxic people will push you to work harder and harder for them, while you completely ignore your own needs. This is exhausting and unacceptable. Create the boundaries you need with these individuals based on your own limits.

Don't Keep Falling for Crisis Situations

Toxic people will make you feel like they need you always because they are constantly in a crisis situation of some sort. It is a neverending cycle. When a person is in a perpetual crisis, it is of their own doing. They often create drama purposely to get extra attention. You may feel guilty for ignoring them, but remember that their being manipulative and not totally genuine.

I am not saying that you can't ever help someone who is going through a hard time. Of course, you can. Just don't start believing that you're responsible for their success or failure.

Focus on the Solution

Toxic individuals will give you a lot to be angry and sad about. If you focus on this, then you will just become miserable. You must focus on the solution, which, in this case, is removing drama and toxicity from your life. Recognize the fact that you will have less emotional stress once you remove this person from your life. If you let them, they will suck away all of your energy.

Accept Your Own Difficulties and Weaknesses

A toxic person will know how to exploit your weaknesses and use them against you. For example, if you are easy to guilt-trip, they will have you feel guilty every time you pull away from them. If you get to know yourself better and recognize these weaknesses, then you can better manage them and protect yourself. This goes along with creating self-awareness, which we discussed in chapter two. When you accept your weaknesses, you can work on fixing them and balance them with your strengths.

They Won't Go Easily

Recognize that a toxic individual may resist being removed from your life.

Actually, if they don't resist, I will be pleasantly surprised. They may throw tantrums, but this is because they can't control or manipulate you anymore. They will even increase their previous tactics with more intensity. It is a trap, and you must not fall for it. Stay firm in your desire to leave and keep pushing forward. If they suck you back in, good luck trying to get out again.

Choose Your Battles Carefully

Fighting with a toxic person is exhausting and usually not worth it. You do not need to engage in every battle with them. They are just trying to instigate you.

Surround Yourself With Healthy relationships

Once you have removed a toxic person, or persons, from your life, then avoid falling into the trap with someone else. Fill your circle with happy and healthy relationships, so there is no room for any toxicity. Always remember the signs of a toxic person, so you can avoid them wholeheartedly in the future.

How to Focus on Self-Care

Now that we have worked to set boundaries and eliminate toxic people from our lives, it is time to focus on ourselves and the self-care we provide. The following are some self-care tips, according to psychologist, Dr. Tchiki Davis, Ph.D.

Pay Attention to Your Sleep

Sleep is an essential part of taking care of yourself. You must make it part of your routine because it will play a huge role in your emotional and physical well-being. There are many things that can wreak havoc on your sleep patterns, like stress, poor diet, watching television, or looking at your phone as you're trying to fall asleep. Think about your night routine. Are you eating right before bed or taking in a lot of sugar and caffeine? Are you working nonstop right up until bedtime? Have you given yourself some time to wind down before going to sleep? All of these factors are important to consider, as they will affect your sleep patterns. If you can, put away any phones, tablets, and turn off the television at least 30 minutes before you plan on going to bed.

Take Care of Your Gut

We often neglect our digestive tract, but it plays a major role in our health and overall well-being. When our gut is not working well, it makes us feel sluggish, bloated, and nonproductive. Pay attention to the food you eat as it will determine the health of your gut. It is best to avoid food with excess salt, sugar, cholesterol, or unhealthy fats. Stick to foods that are high in fiber, protein, healthy fats, and complex carbs. Some good options are whole grains, nuts, lean meats, fruits and vegetables, beans, and fish.

Exercise and Physical Activity Is Essential

Regular exercise is great for both physical and mental health. The physical benefits are obvious. However, many people do not realize that exercise will help the body release certain hormones like endorphins and serotonin. These are often called feel-good hormones because they play a major role in affecting our mood in a positive way. The release of these hormones will give us energy too, which will make us want to exercise more. Once exercise becomes a habit, it will be hard to break. Decide for yourself what your exercise routine will be, whether it's going to the gym, walking around the neighborhood, or playing a game of tennis.

Consider a Mediterranean Diet

While this is not a dietary book, the Mediterranean diet is considered the healthiest diet in the world because of its extreme health benefits. The food groups and ingredients that are used will increase energy, brain function, and has amazing benefits like heart and digestive tract health. The food also does not lack flavor, which shatters the myth that healthy food does not taste good.

Take a Self-Care Trip

Even if you are not much of a traveler, getting away once in a while can do wonders for your mental health. So often, our environment will make us feel stressed out, and it's good to remove ourselves from it for a couple of days. You do not have to take a trip abroad here. Of course, that is certainly an option. A simple weekend trip is perfectly fine. Just get yourself out of your normal routine and be by yourself for a while.

Get Outside

Nature and sunlight can be great medicines. It can help you reduce stress or worry, and has many great health benefits. Doing some physical activity outside, like hiking or gardening, are also great options.

Bring a Pet Into Your Life

Pets can bring you a lot of joy, and the responsibility they come with can boost your self-confidence by having to care for another living creature. Dogs are especially great at helping to reduce stress and anxiety. Animal therapy has been used to help people suffering from disorders lie PTSD, as well.

Get Yourself Organized

Organizing your life and doing some decluttering can do wonders for your mental and emotional health. Decide what area of your life needs to be organized. Do you need to clear your desk, clean out the fridge, or declutter your closet? Do you need to get a calendar or planner and schedule your life better? Whatever you can do to get yourself more organized, do it. Being organized allows you to know how to take better care of yourself.

Cook Yourself Meals At Home

People often neglect the benefits of a good home-cooked meal. They opt, instead, for fast-food or microwave dinners. These types of meals will make you full but will lack in essential nutrients that your body needs. Cooking nutritious meals at home will allow you to use the correct ingredients, so you can feel full and satisfied. Cooking alone can also be great therapy for people.

Read Regularly

Self-help books are a great read. However, do not limit yourself to these. You can also read books on subjects that you find fascinating or books that simply provide entertainment.

Schedule Your Self-Care Time

Just like you would write down an appointment time in your planner, also block out specific times for self-care activities. Stick to this schedule religiously, unless a true emergency comes up. This means that if a friend calls you to go out, you should respectfully decline their request and focus on yourself.

Chapter 4: How to Be Happy Being Alone

The final section of this book will focus on being alone and how to be happy about it. When you start engaging in self-care, you will also be spending much more time by yourself. A lot of people have a hard time dealing with this concept, especially if they're used to being around people all the time. However, for proper self-care, you have to be okay with being alone once in a while.

Accept Some Alone Time

The following are some tips to help you become happy with being alone. Soon, you will realize that your own company is the best kind.

Do Not Compare Yourself to Others

We are referring to your social life here. Do not compare to others, and do not feel like you must live as others do. If you do this, you may become jealous of a person's social circle or lifestyle. It is better to focus on yourself and what makes you happy. If you plan on spending significant time alone, then you cannot pay attention to what other people are doing.

Step Away From Social Media

If strolling through your social media page makes you feel left out, then take a step back and put it away for a while. During self-care moments, you are the focus, not what is happening with others online. Also, what people post on their pages is not always true. Many individuals have been known to exaggerate, or even flat-out lie on social media platforms. You may be feeling jealous or left out for no reason. Try banning yourself from social media for 24-48 hours, and see how it makes you feel.

Take a Break From Your Phone

Avoid making or receiving calls. Let the important people in your life know that you will be away from your phone for a while, so they don't worry. When you are alone, really try to be alone.

Allow Time for Your Mind to Wander

If you feel unusual about doing nothing, it is probably because you have not allowed yourself to be in this position for a while. Carve out a small amount of time where you stay away from TV, music, the internet, and even books. Use this time to just sit quietly with your thoughts. Find a comfortable spot to sit or lie down, then just let your mind wander and see where it takes you. This may seem strange the first time, but with practice, you will get used to the new freedom.

Take Yourself on a Date

You don't need to be with someone else to enjoy a night out on the town. Take a self-date and enjoy your own company for a while. Go to a movie by yourself, stop by a nice restaurant, or just go do an activity you enjoy. If you are not used to hanging out alone, give it some time and you will become more comfortable with it. Take yourself on that solo date.

Exercise

We have mentioned exercise and physical activity a lot, but that's because it has so many great benefits related to self-care. Exercising will uplift your mood, and make it more enjoyable to be by yourself. Those feel-good hormones will provide a lot of benefits during these times.

Take Advantage of the Perks of Being Alone

Some people have spent so much time with other people that they've forgotten the perks of being alone. There are many to consider. First of all, you do not have to ask anyone's permission to do anything; you will have more personal space, can enjoy the activities you want to do, and don't have to worry about upsetting anyone. If you want, you can even have a solo dance party in your living room, Tom Cruise style. There are many advantages to being alone, so use them.

Find a Creative Outlet

It is beneficial to use some of your alone time to work on something creative. This can be painting, sculpting, music, writing, or any other creative endeavors. In fact, you can get out the watercolors and start fingerpainting. Creativity will bring a lot of joy into your life. It will make you happier about being alone.

Take Time to Self-Reflect

Being alone will give you the opportunity to self-reflect on your life. You won't care so much about being alone when you are coming up with important answers to your life.

Make Plans for Your Future

Planning out your life for five or ten years down the line will give you something important to do, and something to look forward to. Alone time is the perfect opportunity to determine these plans.

Make Plans for Solo Outings

Plan your solo outings based on what you like to do, whether it's a farmer's market, hiking, riding your bike, or going camping alone. Mak plans that will excite you, and you will be taking care of yourself while also being okay alone.

There are numerous topics that we went over in this chapter, but they all relate back to one theme: Self-care. Always remember that to take proper care of yourself, you must consider the following ideas:

- Setting Boundaries
- Avoiding and ridding yourself of toxic people
- Focus on yourself and your needs
- Be okay with being alone

Focus on these areas, and you will be demanding your own self-care without ever apologizing for it.

PART IV

Chapter 1: Back to the Basics

When most people think of mindfulness, they envision monks or yogis, sitting cross legged for hours with closed eyes and poised fingers overlooking the Himalayas. Although mindfulness is present in the lives of monks and yogis, what most people don't know is how easy it is to incorporate mindfulness into our everyday lives. As a matter of fact, a mindful state is the most natural and restful state for human beings—a state in which we were all living and moving in as children. If you think back to your childhood, you will likely remember that your concept of time and perception of reality was much different. Most children are very in touch with their emotions, letting them come and go naturally. If a child falls down in one moment and skins their knee, the child will likely begin to cry. However, if a few moments later they are being offered ice cream, their tears will dry, and they will continue on with their day. Mindfulness is the reason children are so in tune with the details of life that adults seem to miss. It is also the reason they are more likely to screech with joy, run around excitedly in enjoyable environments, wake up easily in the morning, and take the time they need to calm down from anger or sadness until the next happy moment arises. Children spend very little time thinking about things beyond the present moment. Even if they have something to look forward to, they are still likely to become invested in the moment at hand, whether that is playing, enjoying time with their parents, or eating a meal. So, what happens as people grow older that brings us away from this natural state of mindfulness?

There are a number of factors that pull people out of the present moment. From the time a child begins elementary school, they are presented with a schedule for the day, which remains relatively the same. Children are expected to remain within the structures presented to them, and the idea of forward-thinking and preparing for the next hour's activity becomes introduced. As they grow, children will likely have more expectations placed upon them, whether those expectations are academic, extracurricular, or within the home. Of course, it is necessary for children to learn how to be responsible and dedicate the time they need to the important things in life. However, as they become further exposed to the constant rush and future-oriented thinking of their parents and teachers, they come to see time as something that no longer belongs to them to fully inhabit.

Furthermore, as people approach teenage and young adulthood, they will begin to face challenges that most children are either shielded from or otherwise unaware of. People become flooded with the pressure to perform well and always be doing more today than yesterday. Although the expectations of cultures and societies vary, we can be sure that people are overwhelmed with the pressure to meet those expectations in order to be considered successful and valid. Once one bar is crossed, another one is waiting, and there is no time to slack. Additionally, the older people become, the more likely they are to be subject to long-lasting pain in their lives. This can come in the form of relationships ending, failing to accomplish something, being mistreated by other people, losing and grieving loved ones, or coming to terms with painful childhood events that did not make sense at the time. Teenagers become increasingly subject to mental health issues as they advance into adulthood, having to face all of the hard realities of the world and still come out on top. People may also be subject to trauma as a result of illness, accident, or abuse. All of these factors are enough to work against people and pull them out of the present moment, either because it is too painful to be there, or because they are simply too distracted.

Human beings experience over 60,000 thoughts per day, but the vast majority are dedicated either to planning for the future or worrying about the past. Becoming overly concerned about the future or steeping in the pains or regrets of the past can increase levels of stress in the body, which makes people more anxious and prone to physical health problems.

The mind naturally wanders, and it is impossible to keep thoughts from coming. Mindfulness is not a tool to eradicate such thoughts, as is the common misconception. Rather, it is a tool through which to acknowledge the thoughts the mind creates, bring attention to them, and allow them to move through. This ultimately brings people into what is happening here and now and gives them more control over their minds and how they orient themselves in their environments.

Because mindfulness is a skill that all human beings are equipped with at our core, it is something that can be re-learned. Just as we exercise our bodies to strengthen our muscles, so we must work to strengthen our brain through mindfulness. The way this strengthening happens is through being aware of thoughts as they arise, then breathing back into the present moment. The more practice is given to returning to the present moment, the stronger the mind will become in remaining in the present more often. Just as the body physically strengthens and becomes healthier over time with exercise, mindfulness exercises can physically change the structure of the brain to make it healthier. Mindfulness activates the positive components of the hippocampus, which is the part of the brain responsible for good things like creativity, joy, and the ability to process emotions. This, in turn, decreases stress levels, depressive tendencies, addictive behaviors, and the fight or flight instinct by shrinking the part of the brain responsible for negative things (the amygdala). Overall, increased mindfulness is the key to a longer, healthier, more creative, and more joyful life.

Chapter 2: Unlocking Your True Purpose Through Mindfulness

Re-centering Yourself

Everyone has days where everything seems to be spinning out of control, and there seems to be no way to manage the chaos. The days where you wake up late, run late to work, spill coffee on your shirt, get cut off on the road, get yelled at by your boss, spend the entire day at work in a confused frenzy, only to come home and bicker with your partner. Since the beginning of time, the human mind has been conditioned to release stress hormones and illicit the fight or flight instinct for the purpose of protection and survival. In the past, this primal instinct was very useful for escaping threats. As times have changed, the threats have become less severe, but the brain's response has remained largely the same. Now, these fight or flight reactions are likely to be triggered by everyday scenarios, such as those previously detailed. The hormone-induced responses that occur when we're stressed out are quick to send us spiraling into emotionally dramatic, and far less peaceful dimensions.

The good news is, mindfulness can be used as a tool for re-centering and gaining control over your anxiety and emotional reactions when you start to feel yourself spiral. Although there is no way to avoid stress and drama in daily life, mindfulness can serve as a shield of calm presence to protect your well-being. If you are preparing to enter a situation that you anticipate could be stressful, like a high-stakes day at work, a scary doctor's appointment, or a difficult conversation with a loved one, it can be incredibly helpful to bring yourself down to a more calm and balanced state in preparation for the stress you are about to deal with. You may find yourself with a racing heart, sweating palms, an unclear head, and the feeling of "butterflies in your stomach." Another area where it is common to feel these physical effects of anxiety is when encountering dramatic situations. Drama can arise tense moments with other people, as well as within the theoretical situations people create for themselves when worrying about what they cannot control (for example, the perception other people have of them, or events that may or may not occur in the future). Giving attention to what is happening in your mind and body and allowing yourself to breathe into the moment can be a total lifesaver in moments of drama or stress. Two to three minutes of deep breathing in your car before going to work, or taking a few deep breaths before reacting in a tense moment, can make a drastic difference in your sense of balance and your ability to deal with stress without launching into fight or flight.

Giving Your Emotions Space

The goal of mindfulness is not to eliminate emotions, but rather, to gain control over the impact they have on how we orient ourselves in the world. It is vital to honor our emotions and give them space to exist and teach us, without letting them seize control. Mindfulness is an excellent tool for giving our emotions space in this way. When an emotion arises, mindfulness gives us a chance to observe that emotion without judgment. In this calm space, we can ask our emotions, "What are you trying to teach me?" We can more clearly discern why we are experiencing a certain emotion, and become in touch with the deeper needs that may have caused that emotion to arise. Just as a child may cry when they need to be nourished our held, we may find ourselves growing angry or agitated when we need support, touch, or self-care. Similarly, we may find ourselves feeling stressed or anxious in scenarios that are subconsciously triggering moments from the past. In these cases, our stress and anxiety are begging us to become in touch with our past self, reminding ourselves that we are safe, and the traumatic moments from the past are over. Once our emotions have been given a non-judgmental space to exist, they can smoothly and peacefully move through the body and be released. This frees us to move from moment to moment like children do, without being constrained by unresolved emotions. Additionally, giving this space to our emotions in mindfulness helps to temper our reactions, which can prevent us from acting out in extreme ways and potentially doing or saying something we regret.

Making Clear Decisions

With the human mind constantly being muddled with thoughts, it can be hard to see things clearly. Sometimes our minds are cluttered by the expectations flying at us from every different direction, or perhaps by our fears of what will happen if things don't go to plan. When it comes to making decisions, we are often faced with numerous options, and it can be difficult to navigate through the chaos in our minds to come to a well thought out resolution. In a distracted, anxious, or removed state, our minds are like a pond on a rainy day—rippling to a point where there is no more clarity. Mindfulness is the calming of the waters, which brings us to a place where we can more clearly think of all possible outcomes of a decision and check in with what we truly need before moving into the next moment.

Keeping Yourself Safe

Although fight or flight instincts originally developed as a way to keep humans safe, in many modern-day scenarios, they do quite the opposite. Let's go back to the example from the beginning of the chapter about the chain of events in a typical chaotic day. If you wake up late in the morning and rush to make your coffee, not paying attention to what you are doing, you run the risk of haphazardly screwing the lid on your to-go cup, then sloshing boiling hot coffee over the edge of the cup and onto yourself as you bolt out the door. Although such a scenario could simply result in a stained shirt, the inattentiveness could have a more drastic effect, such as burning yourself or someone else. Driving to work in a state of panic over running late causes you to be more likely to break the rules of the road— driving too fast, making dangerous decisions when changing lanes, taking turns too fast, running yellow lights just before they turn red, etc. Additionally, the panicked state can lead to anger with yourself or others on the road, which can further impair judgment and put you at greater risk of an accident. Attempting to have a conversation with your boss if you are in fight or flight mode could result in being overly emotional and saying or doing something extreme which could place you at odds within your workplace, potentially even costing your position. Going throughout your day in a frenzy causes you to be less aware of what is going on around you, which can lead to further threats to safety like leaving a burner on, forgetting to eat or drink enough water, or neglecting those in your care (such as pets or children) as a result of your own inner distractions. Finally, as stress from the day carries into the home at the end of the day, it can pose a major threat to relationships. The more stressed out and less clear thinking you are, the more likely you are to say or do something threatening to your partner, to put yourself in an aggressive and volatile situation, and to make brash decisions that have the potential to haunt your future.

Improving Relationships

Just as we must give ourselves space to learn, grow, and process our experiences, we must give that space to those around us as well. When a partner or friend is acting in a way we don't enjoy, mindfulness can allow us to take a step back and look at the situation from a position of empathy. We can allow ourselves to hold space for whatever that person may be going through individually and express our support while also maintaining boundaries and staying in control of what we can. Everyone is deserving of space to be listened to, understood, and supported for who they are. However, it is incredibly difficult to give that space to anyone if it has not been cleared within oneself.

When we operate out of a mindless state, there is hardly any space to meet our own needs and process our own experience, much less to provide that to other people. This can lead us to be closed off to the ones we love, push them away, or act out in anger, selfishness, or aggression. If we have not given space to what is going on within us, we cannot offer full empathy to others. Only 20% of the population is recorded to practice true empathy, which can be linked to the rarity of true mindfulness among adults. Mindfulness allows us to be more present to our own needs in order to hold adequate space for the needs of others as well.

Attention and mutual respect are core elements of every functional relationship. Practicing mindfulness can improve relationships with all the people in our lives by preparing us for every engagement and calming our minds enough to be fully present in the moments we share with others. Mindfulness clears the space for us to listen intentionally to other people and pay more attention to what kind of people they are and what kind of support they need. It allows us to love other people better by increasing our awareness of how they feel most loved. By being present in the moment at hand, as opposed to trapped in the past or future, you are more likely to remember to pick up the phone and give your grandmother a call, to be fully engaged when interacting with your child, or to remember the kind of kombucha your significant other likes best from the store. Not only does mindfulness allow for more meaningful conversations and joyful memories, but it also increases the functionality of our relationships overall so that both ourselves and those we love are feeling fully respected, listened to, and encouraged.

Fostering True Joy

We often hear the term "childlike joy" to describe moments of pure bliss, enthusiasm, and full satisfaction. As people grow into adults, such moments tend to be few and far between, with many remembering the most joyful moments to have been those that occurred in childhood. The expectations of daily life become too much, and most people find themselves trapped in a cycle of constant anticipation. People spend so much time thinking about where they would rather be (on vacation, in bed, enjoying the weekend) that the days melt into each other without us realizing all the moments of our lives we are missing. The biggest societal misconception is that true happiness lies in what we do not yet have. We are flooded with lies such as "Once I can buy this new TV, then I'll be happy," or, "Once I have a partner, then I'll be happy," or, "I'll be happy once I can say I've been to five different countries." Mindfulness abolishes these lies by proving to us that the capacity for true joy lies not in the future but in the here and now. Wherever you are right now, whatever you have, and whichever stage of life you're in, mindfulness reminds you that *this* is your chance to experience beauty and satisfaction like never before. Take time to look at the flowers you did not notice growing in front of your neighbor's house, the complexity of coffee's flavor as it slides down your throat, the way your loved one's eyes crinkle when they smile, the laughter of a child, every intricate flavor of dinner, or the unique people wandering up and down the streets you drive every day to work. It is here that joy resides; all you have to do is be present enough to recognize it.

Chapter 3: Moving Mindfully in Daily Life

Coming to the Present Moment: Daily Guided Mindfulness Meditation With Journaling (Week 1)

Cultivating Mindfulness

This meditation should be done in a space where you feel fully comfortable, safe, and relaxed. Perhaps it is in a corner of your bedroom, in a garden, by your favorite lake, or even in your car. Make sure you can fully relax and avoid distractions. Some people meditate best with instrumental music or nature sounds in the background, while others prefer silence. Feel free to try multiple methods and see which is most soothing to you (this can vary depending on the day). You may do this meditation sitting in a chair, on a mat, or lying flat on your back with your palms up to the sky. You will need to give yourself 5-20 minutes of time to practice, depending on your skill level and current state. If you like, you can set a timer.

Start by coming into the moment with a few deep breaths. Settle into your body and take note of any sensations you feel. If you feel pain, tingling, warmth, or tightness in any part of your body, focus your breath into that space. Imagine any tension unfurling into openness. Notice as your thoughts arise. Take notice of them, then allow them to pass as you come back to the breath. If it is helpful, you can try a breathing pattern in order to culminate focus. To do the 4-4-4 breathing pattern, breathe in for 4 counts, hold for 4 counts, and breathe out for 4 counts. To do the 5-5-7 breathing pattern, breath in for 5 counts, hold for 5 counts, release for 7 counts. Sometimes it helps to imagine breathing in the things you wish to see more of in your daily life (creativity, love, patience, openness) and exhale the negative things (fear, negativity, sadness, stress). Allow yourself to spend a few moments in a more active state of breathing in, releasing, and paying attention to your body.

With practice, you may enter a state where your thoughts slow and you become fully grounded in the present moment. In this state, you are no longer bombarded with thoughts, nor distracted by elements of your environment. It becomes easier to return to the breath. All restlessness and tension in the body seem to melt away, and the mind reaches a flowing, liquified state. There may be days when you cannot enter into this state, and you remain restless throughout the course of the meditation. If this happens, allow it to be that way, observing every thought that arises, then letting it go.

After the time is up, begin to arrive in the moment by moving your body slightly—wiggling your fingers and toes, tensing and releasing your muscles, etc. Next, you're your eyes. Notice how bright and clear the world looks to mindful eyes. Notice the calm, transcendent feeling in your body, and continue to move with it as you go about your day.

Mindfulness Meditation Journal Prompt (Week 1):

What did you feel in your body before beginning? What do you feel now?

Which thoughts continued to arise in your consciousness? Could these thoughts have been trying to teach you something or speak to a deeper need you may have?

How does the world look after opening your eyes? What do you notice?

Come back after going about your day for several hours. Did you bring mindfulness with you into the world? If so, how?

Coming to the Present Moment: Daily Guided Mindfulness Meditation With Journaling (Week 2)

Taking Mindfulness Into the World

This meditation will be done with your eyes open in moments if your daily life. This is not a specific meditation you have to set aside time for, but rather a state you come into. Notice where your attention goes in a given moment. If your attention is drawn to a particular sight, like the nearest tree or a view from the top of a mountain, allow yourself to see it fully. Repeatedly tell yourself, "see, see, see." Breathe as you allow your eyes to truly become totally focused and take in the image fully, allowing it to become a part of your awareness.

If your attention is drawn to an auditory experience, such as the sound of cars on a city street, a rushing body of water, or an internal monologue, give full attention to that thing. Soak in that auditory experience, breathing slowly and telling yourself, "hear, hear, hear."

You may also be drawn to a particular physical or emotional experience within the body. This experience may be positive, like a pleasant bodily sensation or a feeling of joy. It may also be negative, like physical pain, or feelings of anger or feel. Either way, allow yourself to become fully present with what is there, breathing into the experience and seeing what it has to teach you. Breathe into that bodily experience, telling yourself, "feel, feel, feel."

Throughout the day, you'll find that your attention is pulled in various directions. Mindfulness is the choice to tune in to whichever place you're going in a given moment and give full attention to that experience for whatever it is.

Mindfulness Meditation Journal Prompt (Week 2):

How difficult was it to bring mindfulness into your daily life in this way? Where did you face the most challenges?

Did your attention tend towards certain experiences (visual, auditory, bodily) more than others?

Describe a specific moment where you brought mindfulness to your experience and felt truly present. What did you observe?

Coming to the Present Moment: Daily Guided Mindfulness Meditation With Journaling (Week 3)

Mindfulness at Work (or School)

The first part of this meditation should happen in a place outside of work, where you feel safe, calm, and separated from the issues you may face in the workplace. Start by identifying your biggest struggles at work. The journal portion will give you a space to write them down. Do you struggle with productivity? Boredom? Stress? Conflict resolution? Work relationships? Once you have identified your most significant area(s) of struggle, close your eyes and visualize what that unpleasant experience looks like. Perhaps it looks like you, rushing around mindlessly like a bee in a hive, stressed out and too overbooked to step away and breathe because there are more calls to make, more e-mails to send, more things to do. Or, perhaps it is the co-worker, professor, or boss that makes your stomach drop whenever you think about having to interact with them. Perhaps you feel unfulfilled at work and find yourself constantly checking the clock, thinking about the moment you get to leave. Maybe you have so many things to do and no idea where to start, so you waste a lot of time on mindless tasks. Whatever your struggles at work are, use your time and space away from work to safely visualize the situation. Breathe into the mental circumstance.

As you breathe, begin to envision what this experience would look like if it went the way you want it to. Perhaps it looks like the mental clarity that allows you to know exactly what needs to get done and how to make the best possible use of your time. It could be a greater sense of calm and courage when talking with your difficult boss or co-worker and having your message be well-received on their end. It may also be a deeper sense of satisfaction and enjoyment in the work you're doing, providing you the ability to step back and feel a sense of joy with where you're at, without constantly thinking about the next thing. Reframe the moment in your mind until you've created a mental space that feels good. Let yourself sit there, breathing, soaking it in for several minutes.

Once you go into the workplace (or school), you can bring this meditation into your life by going back to the peaceful mental image you've created over and over again. When you begin to feel stressed, bored, anxious, or unproductive, return to the space where you do not feel those things. Bring that energy into your daily work life, and watch how it revolutionizes your experience.

Mindfulness Meditation Journal Prompt (Week 3):

What do you identify as your biggest challenge(s) at work or school?

How does it look when you reframe your struggles to create a positive mental image?

What do you observe about bringing this positive mental image into difficult situations in the workplace or at school?

Mini Meditation Toolbox: 15 Quick and Easy Meditations to Integrate Mindfulness Into Your Daily Life

One-Minute Mindfulness

- Find a space where you can be alone, like on your bathroom break or in your car right before going into work, school, or home at the end of the day.
- Set a timer for one minute
- Close your eyes and focus exclusively on your breathing
- Take notice of the stresses, thoughts, and anxieties that arise, then let them go
- When you open your eyes, notice how you feel de-stressed, clear-minded, and prepared to go about your upcoming tasks and interactions with others

5-Minute Body Scan

- Set a timer for 5 minutes (if needed)
- Close your eyes and take several deep, cleansing breaths. You may use the 4-4-4 or 5-5-7 breathing patterns to deepen the breath
- Begin to bring attention to your body
- Take notice of any sensations that arise-- warmth, tingling, tension, etc.
- Bring your attention to the soles of the feet. Tighten your muscles by curling your toes, then release. What sensations do you feel?

- Continue moving up the body to your calves, hips, abdomen, chest, hands, arms, face, and neck. Observe any sensations that arise, and breathe into those sensations.

- Tighten and release the muscles in each of these areas, allowing any pent-up energy or resistance to be released

- Feel your body become grounded, relaxing completely into the floor, bed, or chair as you come into the present moment in your body and all tension melts away

Mindful Bath/Shower (10-minute meditation)

- As you begin your bath or shower, take a moment to breathe. Remove yourself from the stresses of the day and allow yourself to re-center

- Bring attention to each part of your body as you wash it

- Take notice of any sensations you feel as you move from the soles of your feet to the ends of your hair

- Breathe in the pleasant scent of the soaps and the warmth of the water. Allow yourself to feel clean, warm, and safe.

- As you wash each part of your body, thank it for what it does for you. Then, thank yourself for taking care of your body.

Mindful Morning Routine (15-30 minutes)

- Before getting out of bed, begin to stretch gently, letting thoughts come and go as your mind and body wake up. Do not rush yourself.

- Once you are ready to get out of bed, bring your attention to the space around you and the day ahead. Feel yourself become fully present in that space and prepared to move mindfully through your day

- Pay attention to every move you make, from putting on clothes, to washing your face, to setting the water on the stove to boil.

- Cultivate your awareness for the day ahead by moving slowly and calmly, one task at a time, becoming fully awake to the world

Mindful Housekeeping

- Allow yourself to become focused on the task at hand and only that task. Let every other thing you have to do or think about fade into the background.

- Bring your attention to the breath and the specific way your body moves as you complete a particular task or chore

- Give space to any thoughts or emotions that arise in your consciousness, allowing yourself to process them in a mindful state

Mindful Sit-and-Drink (10-minute meditation)

- Find a calm, quiet space where you can sit and observe the world around you (preferably outside or near a window looking outside)

- Pour a glass of your favorite tea, coffee, or cocktail to enjoy

- Eliminate all distractions. Draw your attention to the intricate flavors of the drink, and the pleasure of pulling something you enjoy into your body

- Take notice of the things happening around you. Find the things in the environment that bring you the most peace, and allow their presence with you to help you calm your mind. Become completely indulged in the moment.

Mindful Scheduling (10-minute meditation)

- Sit down with a pen and paper and center yourself with five deep breaths.

- Think about the days to come. Consider your priorities, remembering that every task is significant and an opportunity for increased mindfulness

- Ask yourself, "Am I giving myself adequate time to bring mindfulness and intentionality into each of these activities?"

- Take notice of any activities you feel you won't be able to be fully present for. Consider taking a thing or two off the list and saving them for a better time.

- Take notice of any feelings of stress, nervousness, or rush you feel in regards to your schedule. Breathe into those feelings.

- As you continue to write your schedule, allow yourself to feel empowered, in control, and prepared to be mindful of everything you are about to do

Mindful Driving

- Leave the house with plenty of time to be relaxed and focused. After entering the car, take a few moments to breathe and center yourself
- Once you start to drive, begin to take note of the things passing by. What do you see today that you did not see yesterday?
- Breathe in your visual surroundings, using them to center and remind yourself: "I am here. I am in this community. This is my life, and I am awake to it."

Mindful Walking (10-20-minute meditation)

- Choose an area where you can relax and bring attention to your surroundings. This can be in a park, in the city, on the beach, in your neighborhood, etc.
- Set out on your walk with no distractions
- Take notice of the things your eyes fall upon. If something specific catches your attention, allow yourself to pause and breathe it in.
- Pay attention to the sounds that surround you, giving yourself space to truly hear them

- Pay attention to the feeling of your feet on the pavement, the swing of your arms at your sides, and the rhythm of your breath

- Let your heart expand in curiosity and openness to whatever is ready to meet you in this space

- Allow yourself to become totally saturated with your surroundings, remembering that everything you see, hear, and feel is a part of you

Mindful Cooking and Eating

- As you enter the kitchen to prepare food, take a moment to center yourself in the moment with a few deep breaths

- Give every moment of the cooking process your full attention, from washing, to cutting, to cooking. Become fully immersed in the process (you can do this even with simple meals, like mindfully spreading peanut butter on bread)

- Breathe loving-kindness into the cooking process, remembering that the food you make will provide nourishment to yourself and others

- Once the food is ready, clear the eating space of distractions. Avoid multi-tasking

- Chew every bite of food 20-30 times, letting yourself be engulfed in the flavor and practicing gratitude for the nourishment

- Walk away from your meal feeling truly nourished and renewed

Mindful Waiting

- The next time you're trying to distract yourself at the doctor's office, the mechanic, or waiting for a friend or colleague to arrive, remind yourself that waiting is one of the most sacred times to engage in mindfulness

- Breathe into the moment, becoming aware of what surrounds you

- Bring awareness to your body. How are you feeling? Take note of any sensations

- Become aware of the thoughts that come once you stop numbing yourself with distractions. What things are running through your mind?

- Pay attention to the deeper thoughts you may have previously been ignoring. Ask yourself what you can learn about yourself and your life, or if there are any actions you need to take.

Mindful Creativity (at least 5 minutes)

- Set aside anywhere from five minutes to several hours of undivided time

- Engage in a creative project like art, writing, dancing, etc.

- Bring full presence to the creative project and try to eliminate all expectations. Allow the moment to carry you.

- Pay attention to how your mind and body react as the moment carries you. How do you feel?

- Examine what you create as a result of this free-flowing creativity

Mindful Play

- Dedicate time each week to doing something truly fun— something that makes you feel like a kid again (climbing a tree, swimming in the lake, drawing with chalk, baking cookies, having a game night, etc.)

- Eliminate all distractions and allow this to be a moment to step away from your everyday life and responsibilities

- Allow yourself to become lost in the childlike joy of play. Laugh loudly, let your body dance, be curious.

- Let the feeling of childlike joy saturate your body and carry this joy with you as you move back into your daily life.

Mindful Movement (10-30 minutes)

- Choose one of your favorite forms of movement (swimming, walking, dancing, going to the gym, etc.) and dedicate at least ten minutes to it

- As you begin to move, establish a deeper sense of body awareness. Pay attention to the feelings in your body as you begin to warm up and exercise

- Pay attention to the way your heart beats, your lungs heave, your face begins to sweat, and your body tingles with the sense of being alive

- Thank your body for all it does for you.

Mindful Listening/Quality Time

- Apply this meditation to any quality time you spend with another person, whether that is grabbing coffee or going for a walk with a loved one, interacting with co-workers, are conversing with the grocery store cashier

- Before interacting with others, bring attention to your levels of empathy. Set the intention to hold space for other people and the moments you share with them

- Eliminate distractions (like technology) and allow yourself to put everything else going on in your life on pause in order to be fully present

- One of the best ways to show love for people and to cultivate personal mindfulness is through mindful listening. Focus all of your attention on the other person and what they are saying. When you ask how their day is going, be present to hear the answer.

- Do not think of what your next move will be, what you will say, or where you will go. Simply be there, showing loving-kindness, holding space, and taking it all in.

Mini Meditation Toolbox: 10 Quick and Easy Meditations to Ease Stress, Depression, Addiction, Anxiety, Pain, Distraction, and Loss Using Mindfulness

Journaling the Consciousness (10-minute meditation)

- Sit down with a journal and a pen and set your timer for 10 minutes
- As thoughts, worries, or emotions arise, immediately write them down. Do not worry about structure, grammar, or content, just write.
- When the time is up, look over what you wrote
- Ask yourself which themes seem to reoccur. Where are you feeling stress in your life? What is occupying most of your mental space?
- Close your eyes and take a few moments to breathe and meditate on the thing(s) that need your attention the most
- Open your eyes. Notice how you feel lighter and in touch with your experience

Distraction Cleanse: Clearing the Space in your Mind

- *Find a quiet place and begin to breathe*
- Ask yourself: "What is distracting me from being present right now?"
- Give space to that distraction, whether it is an invasive thought, personal emotion, or someone else's emotion

- Say to yourself: "I am letting my distractions move through me as I ground myself in the present moment. Nothing is more important than right now."

- Breathe until you feel the distraction melt away into presence and mental clarity.

Re-Writing the Moment: A Short Meditation to Ease Emotional Pain of the Past

- Sit down with a journal and a pen and set your timer for 1 minute

- Take this 1 minute to write down any moment(s) of the past which have caused you a lot of pain

- After the minute is up, choose one of the painful moments, close your eyes, and begin to imagine the moment in a safe way. Be sure to keep breathing.

- When you open your eyes, take your pen and paper and re-imagine the painful moment. What do you wish had happened? How do you wish you could think about the moment now?

- After re-imagining the painful moment, remind yourself that this is a new moment. Everyone has painful memories, but you do not have to stay in spaces of the past, which are painful for you.

- Close your eyes, take a few more breaths, and say to yourself, "I release the pain of that moment of the past. This is a new moment, and I will move with it."

Re-claiming your Inner Power: A Short Meditation to Face Addiction

- Breathe into the moment, allowing yourself to think about the implications your addiction has on your life

- Without judgment, question your addiction. Ask yourself, "What has been left empty in me that I am trying to fill with this?" Listen for any emotions or past experiences of trauma, grief, or abandonment that arise. Allow them to be there.

- Say to yourself, "Now that I understand the root of my addiction, I can begin to be set free."

- With closed eyes, begin to breathe. With each breath, imagine your addiction's hold on you weakening and weakening until eventually, you have been released.

- Move forward into your life with the idea that your addiction's hold on you is loosening, day by day.

Letter to the Lost: A Short Meditation to Address Grief and Loss

- Sit down with a journal and a pen and take five deep breaths to bring you into the moment

- Allow someone you have lost to come to mind. This can be a relationship that has ended, someone who has died, etc.

- Close your eyes and breathe into the space this person has left empty within you. Allow yourself to experience any emotions that arise.

- When you open your eyes, take a few minutes to write what you wish you could have said to that person

- After you have finished your letter, close your eyes again. Tell your grief that it is okay for it to be there. With every breath, imagine yourself moving forward in your life, released from every regret you may have with someone you've lost

In with The Positive, Out with the Negative: A Short Breathing Technique

- Find a comfortable space and prepare to use the 5-5-7 breathing technique
- Breathe in for five counts and think of something positive you want to bring into this moment (kindness, peace, wisdom, etc.)
- Hold for five counts, allowing this positive thing to fill your body
- Exhale for seven counts, thinking of something negative you want to release from your body in this moment (stress, tension, selfishness, etc.)
- Begin again with a second emotion. Do this as many times as you like until you feel well-equipped with positive emotions and have released all negative ones

Space to Breathe: A Short Meditation to Gain Control over your Anxiety

- When you begin to feel anxious, step away, take a breath, and ground yourself in the moment by finding one thing you can see, one thing you can hear, and one thing you can feel. Focus deeply on each thing.

- Allow your anxiety space to exist. Remember, anxiety is the reaction your emotional brain has when it senses a threat. You can bring yourself back from catastrophe mode by using the rational brain to repeatedly remind yourself: "I am safe. I am in control. I am capable of being calm."

- Keep breathing and saying these rational-brained affirmations until you begin to feel your anxiety melt away

- Move into the next moment feeling calm, anxiety-free, and empowered

Emotion Coding: A Short Meditation to Bring you in Touch with your Emotions

- Find a quiet, comfortable place where you can easily connect with yourself

- Close your eyes and breathe deeply (you may use a breathing pattern if desired)

- Begin to travel inwards. Say to yourself, "I am ready to accept the emotions that are here."

- Wait patiently, focusing on the breath, and observing every emotion that rises to the surface.

- When an emotion arises, ask yourself a series of questions:

  1. "Is this emotion mine or someone else's?"
  2. "Does this emotion serve me or hold me back?"
  3. "What is this emotion trying to teach me?"
  4. "Should I release this emotion or put it into action?"

- When it comes to answering each question, listen to your intuition. The answers to each question are already within you. Do not question your natural answers.

- If you are being told to release an old or negative emotion, or an emotion that belongs to someone else, breathe and imagine it melting away with every exhale

- If you are being told to foster a positive emotion or a strong emotion that can create positive change in the world, sit with that, breathing, and being open to how that emotion can be useful.

The "I Love..." Gratitude Meditation (2-minute meditation)

- Find a private space, preferably one in front of a mirror

- Start a timer for 2 minutes

- For two minutes, speak out loud sentences of gratitude beginning with the words "I love…" ("I love my partner," "I love coffee," "I love my cat," "I love sunflowers," "I love my mom," "I love to dance," "I love that I am healthy,").

- Say as many things as you can, one after the other. Do not think too much, simply let the things you love flow from your lips

- When the timer goes off, look in the mirror and say "And I love you," to yourself

- Feel the magic of gratitude transforming your life, your self-confidence, and your ability to be mindful

The Mindful Manifestation: A Short Meditation to Manifest what you Want in Life

- Sit down with a journal and pen

- Begin to cultivate mindfulness by bringing attention to your breath and any sensations in your body

- Ask yourself the question: "What do I want most in life?"

- As the answers start to come, open your eyes and begin to write your desires with the words "I manifest..." in front of them ("I manifest empathy." "I manifest peace of mind." "I manifest protection." "I manifest safety." "I manifest love." "I manifest awareness." "I manifest wisdom." "I manifest pure joy.")

- With each manifestation, close your eyes, and say it to yourself at least three times. Feel this manifestation become a part of your reality.

PART V

Chapter 1: Is This for You?

Before we start this adventure, we have to ask, who is this intended for? The short answer is that it is for everyone who wants to make a positive change in their lives. The key word there is "want". This is ultimately a choice. You must establish your own journey as the techniques exemplified in this book are just practices. There is no set number of meditation sessions that will unlock mindfulness. The practice of these techniques only increases the chances of your own self-discovery. Your willingness to find that goal is the only way these practices will be effective.

This may seem confusing or even overwhelming, but it should be celebrated! You have made a choice to better your life. You possess the bravery to examine yourself in your own state. You are already stronger for it. There is value in yourself and your life and you have already made the decision to discover yourself at your most honest, happiest state and to continue to not only endure but thrive in a world made by your own choices. The biggest step is the first one, and that step is already behind you. It is time to breathe a sigh of relief, to feel accomplished. The worst part of your journey is behind you.

Now that you have made the first step, where do you go? Obviously, the answer is your own choice. The practices in this book are merely there to help you along the way. This may or may not be a path that you have previously gone down, so use these techniques to guide you in your own journey. Look at this book as a toolkit. There is nothing in these pages that will assume a role of authority over you. That is the beauty of free will! You are free to explore at your own pace in your own order.

"Often, it's not about becoming a new person, but becoming the person you were meant to be, and already are, but don't know how to be."

— Heath L. Buckmaster, Box of Hair: A Fairy Tale

You have already made the most important step, and that step is the one that separates you from your furthest setbacks. There is already so much distance between where you were and where you are now. It is now possible to look back and accept yourself. Standing where you are now, it is possible to see your own worth. You are not your setbacks, and you are not your failures. In fact, you might be the most interesting person you know!

Chapter 2: Your Toolbox, DBT

The goal of Dialectical Behavior Therapy (DBT) is to separate you from behaviors that are harmful to yourself and others and replace them with meaningful habits. Now that you have taken your first step and have separated yourself from your setbacks, you can go even further and discover what it is that makes you truly happy on your own. Finding that you do not live to continue harmful behaviors but discovering and tailoring habits that will enhance the life that you are choosing to live will fill you with serenity and self-love, and it will be all the more meaningful because they will be your own interests and not the consequences of your setbacks. Honestly, how exciting is it to really discover the real you? Someone that you may have never met or may not have seen in a long time and neither has anyone else, a brand-new person who has been there all along.

The defined objectives of DBT is obviously a little more clinical. It includes Mindfulness, Distress Tolerance, Interpersonal Effectiveness, and Emotion Regulation. How does this relate to you, though? How do these skills fit into your new and exciting life? Remember that the goal of this kind of therapy is not to overtake your life, but to be there alongside it to help you discover what it is that makes you the real you.

Mindfulness is not a skill set, more so a state of being. Mindfulness is being aware of the present, in the present, and not to be overwhelmed by what is going on around you. It is an awesome way to be and reinforces who you are because only you have a mind like yours. Whenever you are using your senses to become directly aware of your present state of being, you are being mindful. Mindfulness is also exercised like a muscle. It is something that we all possess, but few regularly practice. Although that statement may not be true for long. There is a growing interest in meditation and a growing awareness of the importance of remaining mindful in every aspect of life from personal to even business. If you were to practice it, you will discover that the feeling of mindfulness becomes stronger the more you exercise that mental muscle. Focus and personal honesty will become stronger as you develop along this path. It is an exciting tool of self-discovery and one that will be explored upon later in this book.

Distress Tolerance is a measurement. It is your ability to accept distress that cannot be changed. Emotional pain is measured on a different scale altogether from physical pain, but it can be just as, or even more, damaging. The real skill here is learning how to find your own way around the distress and accept what you are unable to change. Practicing mindfulness will help you to separate yourself from distress factors but coming to terms with the reality of these stressful situations will no longer be a roadblock, but a defining challenge that will make you stronger and give you skills for future distress management.

"Grant me the serenity, to accept the things I cannot change; courage to change the things I can; and wisdom to know the difference."

Learning the difference between what you can and cannot control is paramount. Once you have accepted the reality of a stressful situation that you cannot control, you cease to try to change it but begin to find a path to live around or through it. Sometimes, the energy spent trying to change an unchangeable situation is more stressful than the original event! You owe it to yourself to not harm yourself. There are even times when the situation only seems to be so stressful because you have spent all of your energy and effort trying to change it instead of taking a step back and accepting it for what it is. You could even come to realize that the situation is more benign than how you have built it up to be inside your head. Sometimes, you can even find a way to turn it into a positive situation! You will never be able to do any of that if you are too busy stressing about the original situation, though.

Interpersonal Effectiveness will help you to build and maintain important relationships, including the one you have with yourself, as well as help you to define priorities and to arrange them in a sensible manner to live your new life the most effective. The clinical method is through the acronym DEAR MAN:

- **D**escribe the current situations
- **E**xpress your feelings and opinions
- **A**ssert yourself by asking for what you want, or by saying no
- **R**eward the person – let them know what they will get out of it
- **M**indful of objectives without distractions (attack the problem, not the person)
- **A**ppear effective and competent
- **N**egotiate alternative solutions

These are effective and healthy steps for conflict resolution and a great tool to have in mind to keep your communication on track and working towards an agreeable solution.

Respect is a trait valued by everybody in one way or another. Respect is earned and kept and can encourage stronger relationships with the important people in your life. Speaking in a respectful tone will lead you to your interpersonal goals in a way than getting agitated towards that person, situation, or even yourself. Self-respect is the true basis of interpersonal respect. Have you ever heard that you must learn to love yourself before you can love another? This is because you define for yourself, and exemplify to others, what respect means to you. How you treat yourself will set the standard for how others will feel that they can treat you. A person who dresses nice and speaks warmly with peers will garner more respect than a person who shows little care for how they want to be treated. Self-respect is important, and you deserve it! You are already stronger for having taken this journey and your story is one that no one else has. You are worthwhile, interesting, and unique. Taking good care of yourself will tell others that you are a person who warrants respect. Another acronym that is helpful about self-respect is FAST.

- **F**air to myself and others
- No **A**pologies for being alive
- **S**tick to values (do not do anything you will regret later)
- **T**ruthful without excuses or exaggeration

You have heard the Golden Rule; treat others as you would like to be treated yourself. Well, that rule works the other way as well! Treat yourself as you would treat others. You deserve the same respect that you would show to others, so do not count yourself out or make sacrifices that make you feel uncomfortable. Be fair to yourself!

If you find that you apologize unnecessarily, stop it! Sometimes, people will tell you that you apologize too much, which only make you feel uncomfortable. You do not have to apologize for anything that you are not truly sorry for. You occupy the same space as your peers and you deserve the same level of respect.

What are your values? Do you know? In your current stage of rebuilding and discovery, your values may change, or you may discover that you have been violating your own values for a long time. With a renewed respect for yourself and a bright new path ahead of you, you are most likely to find out what is truly important to you. Find your core values and remember that you deserve respect. You do not have to apologize for your values and you do not have to compromise your values. Make your identity known and remember that you are valid.

Once you know who you are, what you value, and the fact that you deserve and possess self-respect, honesty becomes easy. You do not have to fabricate yourself to fit in or hide any unsavory traits that you may think that you possess. Your peers will respect an honest you. Honesty to yourself and others is the pinnacle of freedom. You are who you are and who you are is a strong, healthy, and an interesting person! Half-truths and flat out lies do little more than create stress for everyone involved, including yourself. A person with self-respect does not need to create an identity that they do not own. Breathe and relax because you are you!

Chapter 3: Finding Yourself through Mindfulness

Discovering yourself is exciting! It's a journey that is enviable. We have already defined mindfulness, so the next step is to discover how it is practiced and define what your individual goals are. It is important to remember to constantly ask yourself what you want to find in this book. Your individual goals are the goals of this text. What practitioners of mindfulness usually find is greater fulfillment, a deeper understanding of their selves, positive behavioral changes, and more importantly, less suffering.

As you continue down this path, it is important to remember what your truest intentions are because doubts will surface. Mindfulness will need to be practiced and exercised like a muscle. Minds are messy, prone to wandering, prone to doubt, and everyone examines themselves much harsher than their peers would. In the last chapter, you discovered what your values are and who you are as a person. You discovered that self-respect is worth having. Now, it is time to reinforce what you know about yourself and what you want to explore.

Before we get to the actual practices, it is important to note that the path to mindfulness is not linear. It is a little different for everyone and the only outside guide is a collection of experiences from others. The true guide is yourself. Do not fret. Do not succumb to doubt because you may or may not discover a path differently or find a truth not listed in this book. No one can know you as well as you can. Instead of reveling in the doubt or confusion, be excited! You are the first to discover your exact path and you are the first to find your own unique solutions to your setbacks.

At the same time, you may discover that these goals are even connected! As you discover greater fulfillment, you may connect it to lesser suffering, and from there, you may find that you exhibit better behavior and more success in your relationships. Understand that practicing separateness from your suffering could lead to accepting validation from your own positive thoughts and energy.

The most obvious exercise for practicing mindfulness is meditation. It is important to note that meditation is not passive. It is not simply sitting and relaxing with your eyes closed. It is an active exploration of your mind while providing yourself with the least resistance to your own self-discovery. You may not just drop right into it during your first session. An unpracticed mind has never explored in that way. You may not know how to look inward as your senses and instincts are conditioned to look outward for stimulation.

First, you must separate yourself from your reactions. You must understand what your automatic reactions to a stimulus such as stress and joy are and be aware of yourself at the moment that you act automatically. You are not your feelings. You are not your reactions. Imagine you are on the side of a road watching traffic pass back and forth. Every car is a stimulus, feeling, or reaction. You are separate from them and you must merely make a mental note of it, and then let it pass. Be aware of their existence and acknowledge them, but do not react to them. Eventually, your mind will become more still.

Another example is to imagine your mind like a still pool of water. Every thought and stimulus is a pebble dropped in that pool. Those pebbles create concentric ripples that expand outward, and then even out. If you reach into the water to grab that pebble, you will only create a splash and larger ripples. Eventually, the pebbles will slow, and your quietest realizations and truths will surface. Do not fear! This is your truest self. This is exciting and another great achievement along with your journey to a more peaceful and successful you. After those truths have passed without judgment, your pool of water will fall even more still. You will experience true serenity and discover the most honest definition of a quiet mind. This is peace.

To practice meditation, you must first dedicate time and space to your session. You do not need a special pillow or certain music or any equipment whatsoever, just time and space to practice. Sit in a comfortable position that you will not stress to maintain and close your eyes. Next, just acknowledge the moment as it is. Observe it without judgment or interaction. Just simply be in the moment without exerting effort or energy towards it. Pay attention to the sensations of air passing through your nostrils or the presence of sound in your ears. Let the moment pass through you as you sit peacefully in it. The goal is not simply to be calm, it is to be aware of the moment as it is happening right now without interaction or judgment. The next step is not so much a step, but a reassurance. Judgments will rise. It is inevitable, especially when you are first practicing. Remain calm and remain practicing. Do not succumb to doubt or frustration. Simply make a note of it, and let it pass. This is an excellent practice for learning how to move on from frustration or feelings of grudge in your waking life. If your mind wanders too far off of your initial concentration, keep returning to the sensation of your breath. Focus on the gentle sensation of the in and out of your breathing. Simply be in your awareness.

Meditation is a proven method to reduce stress, increase clarity, and can even positively rearrange your brain chemistry! You will notice your brain will have less chatter in your normal life, and you will be less prone to anxiety. It is a great practice for finding a "third way" around a conflict. It can even open up your creativity and lower your heart rate and blood pressure. As I have mentioned before, it has even begun to appear in modern business practices. Some higher up CEOs have adopted this daily practice to increase their creativity and productivity and reduce their stress level in the fast-paced environment that is business. Everyone from athletes to political figures to your average working man benefits from this simple practice.

If you chose to partake in this particular practice, you are unlikely to regret it. The next chapter will focus on advanced meditation techniques for when you discover that you like this new calmer, more focused you!

Chapter 4: Taking Mindfulness to the Next Level with Advanced Meditation Techniques

If you have chosen to give meditation a try, then congratulations! You should feel proud of yourself for having the courage to try something new. You should feel reinforced in your feelings of solidity in your new and healthy life. You have made an actual effort and have taken real-life actions! This is another moment to look at just how far you have come. How has meditation affected your life already? Do you feel a renewed clarity? This chapter will show you advanced techniques that you can practice to further expand your meditation practices.

An easy form of meditation that you can incorporate in your daily life is called a Walking Meditation. Obviously, this can be done simply while walking, or any form of ambulation that you use to get around. It is an action that you do naturally and has been for years. You probably learned how to walk before you learned how to read! This kind of easy, almost automatic and steady movement is a perfect environment to study your meditation practices.

First, you must stand up straight. Keep your back straight as you practice this. It is important to find the posture that is comfortable and promotes easy steps and focus. Next, place your hands together just above your belly button with your thumbs curled in towards your palms. This position promotes a comfortable posture that brings your focus to your center. Your arms are not swaying, and you feel self-contained and comfortable. Now, let your gaze drop slightly. This will also allow you to focus while being aware of where you are walking to. Just like with normal sitting meditation, try not to get lost in outside stimuli, just simply make a note of them and continue on with your focus inwards. Now, you are ready to take your first step. In the last section, I mentioned that breathing could be used to bring your focus back to your center. In this exercise, you will use your steady footfalls to create a rhythmic cadence for you to keep your central focus on. Notice, without interacting, the sensation of the ground on your feet (or whatever mode of transportation that you would use to get around on your own). Notice as the ground rolls from the back to the front of your foot. Notice the gentle bounce of your body as you move along. Now, do the same with the next step and the next. Make sure to walk at a slightly slower pace than usual. It is not necessary to move ridiculously slow, just make sure that it is at a pace where you are able to focus on your gentle and rhythmic movements and still move along at a comfortable speed.

Benefits of this style of meditation are that it allows you to further exercise your focus outside of the room or environment that you have become comfortable meditating in. It allows you to start connecting that focus to your daily life as you practice maintaining that focus during the natural and unpredictable distractions that occur just in a day out. You will also begin to appreciate the seemingly mundane aspects of your day, bringing focus and renewed eyes to aspects of this wonderful life that may have gone unnoticed or underappreciated previously. A cloud moving in front of the sun might bring certain effects to your attention like the changing colors or temperature of this temporary state. You might find a renewed appreciation for the sun and life in general. A gentle breeze might remind you of how temporary forces in your life are. A passing conversation might show you how calm, focused, and centered you are feeling in the moment versus how frantic and anxious the average person is in their daily life. You will discover all of these things while keeping your focus centered. It is important to not react to any of their thoughts, just simply recognize the existence of these thoughts, and let them pass naturally on their own. Bringing your meditation practices from your sterile environment to the waking world is an excellent practice for learning how to maintain and call upon this state of focus when there are events in your life that may be exciting or stressful.

The next technique is quite the opposite. Instead of walking, this technique is most effective while laying down, but it can be done in a sitting position. It is called a Body Scan, and it is used to focus on your physical wellbeing. It gives the sensation of infusing your body with a healing breath.

First, you must sit or lie in a comfortable position. Do not pick a position or surface that will become uncomfortable or distracting during your meditation. Once you are in a good position, place your hands on your stomach in the same manner in which you did during the Walking Meditation, just above your belly button in a comfortable position that brings your focus to the center of your body in a full rest. Once you are in this position, you might find it easier to focus if you close your eyes. Now, take a few deep breaths. Take note of the moment as you are in it, just like you have practiced in the basic meditation technique. Then bring your attention to your body. Notice the sensation and pressure of the floor or chair on your back or legs. Keep taking deep breaths, but this time, notice the invigorating life that fills your body when you inhale deeply and then feel a deeper sense of relaxation on every exhale. Fall deeper and deeper into your focused state with each incremental breath. You may start to notice more minute sensations such as your pulse under your skin, or little hairs standing up on your arm as your body becomes more relaxed and focus.

Now, bring your focus to your stomach area. If your stomach is tense, let it loose. You might even notice that your entire body relaxes as you release the tension in your stomach. Shift your focus from your stomach to your hands just above that area. See if you can allow your hands to soften even more. Feel your body relax even another level. Now, bring your focus to your arms. Let the tension loose in your shoulders. Let the tension loose in your biceps and forearms. After that, it is time to bring your focus to your neck. Let the muscles in your neck relax. It is perfectly acceptable to let your body shift as your muscles become systematically more relaxed. It is almost bound to happen as you are achieving new levels of relaxation. How relaxed you are now will make your initial assessment when you first lied down seem so distant.

After you have relaxed your neck, then it is time to focus on your jaw. Let that tension go. In your waking life, the average person carries extra tension especially in their jaw, shoulders, and fists without even realizing it. You might perceive yourself as relaxed when in actuality; you are much tenser than what is comfortable. This is one of those realizations that you come across through meditation that is an invaluable lesson that you have taught yourself. After you have rolled your relaxing focus over your entire body, take a mental snapshot of your body as a whole. Notice your body in the same way that you notice passing thoughts in the basic meditation technique. You may realize that your body is yours, but it is not you. Your body is a vessel and a tool for who you really are. That separation is important when you practice meditation. It is what allows you to examine thoughts without attachment. Take one more deep breath and allow your eyes to open, feeling a new sense of invigoration and relaxation.

Congratulations! With these three meditation techniques; the basic meditation, the Body Scan, and the Walking Meditation, you are able to perceive and react to thoughts and stimuli within your mind, your body, and your world in a healthy way. There is nothing that you should not be able to process using these techniques. You now have the tools to tackle any hardships along your journey. On top of that, you now have a new perspective that is exciting to explore as you find new hobbies, relationships, and life choices. Now even simple tasks like breathing, walking, or even just existing can be healing and full of positive energy!

The next chapter will focus on processing negative thought patterns in a healthy way. Now that you have this new perspective and new tools, it should be easy to separate yourself from negative thoughts that may surface from your past or present life. Do not fear! You are ready. You are stronger than you have ever been, and you can tackle any setbacks you have experienced, or are currently experiencing. Take a moment to celebrate where you are versus where you have been!

Chapter 5: Using Your New Tools to Process Negative Emotions

Negative emotions will occur. It is the inevitability that comes with the endless possibilities of life. You cannot reasonably expect to live your entire life and never feel sad, hurt, angry, betrayed, embarrassed, or any other emotion that can be perceived as negative. In this chapter, we will review the skills that you have learned to more effectively process your emotions when an inevitably negative emotion occurs. Through Dialectical Behavior Therapy, Emotion Regulation breaks down into three goals.

1. Understand one's emotions
2. Reduce emotional vulnerability
3. Decrease emotional suffering

The first step begins with a simple truth, and that is emotions are not bad. Even negative emotions are not something to just be avoided. It is impossible, and unhealthy to attempt, to avoid every negative emotion that you will come across in your life. Attachment to negative feelings is what causes real suffering. You learned from the last two chapters how to separate yourself from thoughts and emotions. You simply must acknowledge the emotion and/or event, and then let it pass. It is important to acknowledge these emotions, though. Try to define your emotions clearly. Using phrases like "I feel bad" does not give a clear understanding of how you are feeling. Instead of "bad", expand on that. Pinpoint it by saying you feel frustrated, depressed, anxious, or angry. Understanding what and how you are feeling is integral to processing those feelings. It is also important to understand the difference between primary and secondary emotions.

Primary emotions are reactions to an outside stimulus, and secondary emotions are reactions to those primary emotions. For example, if you felt depressed later about being too angry at a friend, then anger would be the primary emotion while depression would be the secondary emotion. The secondary emotion is a judgment of the primary emotion. Learning how to acknowledge emotions without judgment is essential because secondary emotions are destructive. Also, learning how to process negative events without succumbing to negative emotions is very important. Maybe being angry at the friend was not the proper response when you could have used the DEAR MAN acronym in the second chapter of this book to properly resolve that event and those feelings in a way that would solve the issue and be beneficial to both you and your friend. Remember that emotions are not your identity. Emotions are there just to alert you to stimuli that are beneficial or problematic. How you process and express these emotions is entirely up to you.

Reducing emotional vulnerability will increase the stability of your emotions, simply put. In DBT, the methods for reducing emotional vulnerability is through action. It will teach you to create positive habits and experiences to balance out the negative feelings you might be feeling. An easy acronym to remember for this is PLEASE MASTER.

PL – represents taking care of your physical body and reducing or treating illness

E – eat a balanced diet

A – is for avoiding alcohol and drugs, which can only heighten or fabricate negative feelings

S – Sleep. It is important to get regular sleep

E – The last E is for exercise. Much like meditation, it will increase in benefits the more you practice.

MASTER – This one is the fun one. Master positive activities to increase your sense of well-being and accomplishment.

Your health affects your emotional state. This ties into the self-respect section that we talked about in the second chapter. You will feel much better physically and emotionally if you raise your standards of how you treat yourself. Getting regular sleep, exercise, and only treating your body and yourself to healthy food and activities will do absolute wonders for your confidence. This also includes avoiding alcohol and drugs. It is too easy to mask feelings with these substances, and as we have learned, that is not a healthy way to process those emotions. Avoiding emotions, especially with mind-altering substances, does not make those emotions go away. It is not a permanent solution, it only encourages you to chase that perceived temporary safety from those emotions while your body is developing an addiction to the actual substance. It is a trap and can only work to undo all of the work that you have already accomplished. Treat yourself better than that because not only do you have self-respect, but you deserve it.

Now, I am going to circle back to the PL portion of the PLEASE MASTER acronym. After you understand the steps necessary for taking care of your body, you will understand that it is important to monitor your body as a whole. This includes taking care of illnesses when they arrive. Illness is another inevitability of life. Much like emotions, it is important to process them in a healthy manner to avoid further damage. You deserve to live in a healthy body and you owe it to yourself to take care of yourself. Living in a healthy body will give you peace of mind. Knowing that at the end of the day, you are physically feeling healthy will put other situations in perspective and it will be one more positive that you can weigh against negative emotions when they occur. Along with exercise and meditation, you can choose to MASTER other positive activities in your life. Developing or rediscovering a hobby is exciting and can give new meaning and a new sense of accomplishment in your life!

After you have learned these skills, you are ready to learn how to decrease emotional suffering. In DBT, it is comprised of only two skills: Letting go and taking opposite action.

Letting go refers to what we have already learned, by using our mindfulness to process emotions in a healthy way by letting them pass without developing secondary emotions to attach to the primary emotions. Taking opposite action means engaging in actions that are in direct contrast to the negative feelings that you are experiencing. For example, instead of crying when a feeling of depression is acknowledged, try to stand straight, speak confidently, and react to the stimulus or event in a healthy way. This is not to ignore that emotion. It is an exercise to lessen the length and severity of the emotion. It is important to acknowledge emotions, but that does not mean that you have to be subordinate to them. You do not need to let emotions control how you think and act. It can also give you a new perspective on a situation that you may have reacted automatically too.

With these skills, coupled with the skills you have learned in the previous few chapters, you can process emotions internally in your mind, body, and everyday life and also express those emotions after you have processed them. Even more to add to that, you have developed a renewed sense of self-respect through self-care and new or rediscovered hobbies. You are now taking steps to replace negative habits and feelings with positive feelings and activities you enjoy and that are uniquely representative of you! You may start to feel that you are meeting the real you, a more positive and honest version of yourself, doing things that you enjoy.

Chapter 6: Defining Your Goals, Your Values, and Yourself

Now, instead of learning something new, it is time to reassess yourself after what you have already learned. Do you remember those goals and values that you defined for yourself at the beginning of this book? Well much like how we discovered new levels of relaxation during the Body Scan meditation, it is time to discover new levels of yourself. Maybe after you have practiced meditation and studied the different goals of DBT, your renewed sense of self and awareness can further sharpen your goals and expectations from your new life. It is even possible that you have already achieved and mastered some of your goals. If you have, then congratulations! It is time to reassess what is important to you and what you can get out of this book. If you have not achieved any of your goals yet, then do not worry! Hopefully, you have set expectations at a reasonable level and you are mindful of what you are able to achieve within yourself. It is good to have both long-term and short-term goals. It is important, even, to balance both so you are able to celebrate achievements along the path to a life-affirming goal that you may not have been able to achieve without taking that all important first step along this journey.

Each new skill you learn is a skill you would not have had if you would have maintained your negative feelings and habits. There are questions for you now that only you can answer. How is it that you feel? How do you feel in a general sense of wellbeing? How far along do you think you have traveled? You are most likely aware of your progress and it is good to celebrate along the way. These steps you are taking are not steps that any one person could take for you, no matter how influential or qualified. Just like how meditation and mindfulness is a study of you, the steps you have taken are entirely unique to you.

Having said all of that, it is important to allow positive feelings to be acknowledged and witnessed. Many have a hard time accepting themselves in their own achievements. Judgments upon oneself can absolutely be the harshest. It is easy for faults and negative feelings to seem large and overwhelming when you are standing so near to them. These negative feelings cause you to stress and can be impossible to simply ignore. This is why we learn to process those feelings and resolve them instead of trying in vain to ignore them. An unresolved negative feeling can trigger a survival response, which is why it is impossible to ignore said feelings. In this way, unresolved negative feelings make it near impossible to accept positive feelings about yourself.

Your body does not feel the need to react to positive feelings because it feels that the situation is resolved because it ended on a satisfying conclusion. Your body will tell you that your time and effort need to be spent resolving those negative feelings because they are triggering a survival response in you. Now that you have learned how to bring negative feelings to a positive and productive conclusion, it is now possible to accept your positive traits and individuality. It is even possible to meet yourself without those impossible stresses in your life. How exciting and life-affirming is that! How much better off are you now in relation to how you were before you took this journey?

Now, that you know your goals, and you know yourself, what are your values in your new life now? What have you learned that you could possibly maintain, or even teach others? Maybe you recognize the work that you have put in and are starting to recognize the results of hard work. Maybe you value patience and understanding because practicing meditation has taught you how to discover feelings that were always there, just buried. All this book can do is speculate and give examples to what you may be feeling. It is your unique journey that is your real teacher. You have taught yourself how to heal. You have taught yourself how to take the first step, and you have taught yourself how to recognize greatness within yourself.

Are there people in your life who would be proud of you for where you are now? If so, you should greet them and share your renewed sense of pride and clarity with them. It is reaffirming of your own sense of accomplishments to have it validated by those you love, those you admire, and those you respect. Sometimes, it can give a new perspective to emphasize with someone else and share a joyful feeling with them. You are no longer in a cave of your own misjudgments, both internal and external. You have established yourself out in the light. You can walk among the world with your head high instead of living in the past and inside of your own head. You see the world for how it actually is and not through the lens of prior transgressions or feelings of worthlessness. It is even possible to look back at how you used to exist and treat yourself and separate yourself enough from it that you can even brush it off. That is not you anymore. You are the real you now. You are the you that you were meant to be, a much happier and more honest you who recognizes real emotions instead of perceived injustices to yourself.

Chapter 7: Living in the Positive!

Now that you have created a positive atmosphere for your mind to exist in, you are probably feeling a new motivation and longing to explore the world in your new self. What do you do with all of this motivation? It is important to put this good energy to use as to not fall back into negative habits that your old self has come to reinforce. You are at a crucial step where you should give great importance to channeling this positive energy into positive habits.

Something that you can do for yourself is to continue to practice meditation and exercise. Your new positive life starts at your core. Your core being yourself. You have learned a renewed sense of self-respect and discovered some deep insight into yourself. Now, it is time to maintain it. You can continue to live positive as long as you take care of yourself. Imagine yourself in a fancy car. It can look nice on the outside, but if the engine is not kept in good condition, it will not function as intended. Every new positive action starts with a sense of wellbeing.

Other ways to maintain your emotional stability through practice is to find a creative outlet for your feelings. If you feel that you are the creative type of person, then you may already have some of these hobbies. You may even have hobbies that you have not visited in a long time. Picking up an old hobby can help you connect with who you were before you found yourself down a darker path. It can give you a sense that you are picking up where you left off and reassure you that this you is the real you. If you are not a creative person or have not found an interest in a hobby, then do not worry! Another way that you can strengthen your mental focus and reinforce this new positive you are to learn. Reading is a proven method to increase cognitive faculties and helps you to directly discover interesting perspectives that you may not have come to on your own independently. Maybe, you will even discover ways to learn about aspects of your life that you have put on hold. Projects and promises made to others and you can now be fulfilled because you are now breathing easy and have a new motivation for life.

Great! Now that you have a healthy and positive sense of wellbeing, you can further reinforce your new positive life by engaging in productive social activities. Before I get into examples of this, I want to further explore the benefits.

Giving back to your community outwardly shows that you want to be engaged with society. You recognize yourself as a part of a whole and you are devoid of an ego that alienates you from your peers. It is not a struggle for your individuality though; you have already explored and defined yourself to yourself. Now, it is time to show who you are to the world! A person who lives inside of their own negative thought patterns does not want to be a part of society. They will build their own mental walls to keep themselves from embarrassment, anger, shame, or any other negative thought patterns associated with social interaction. Maybe they feel that society owes them something. An overinflated ego is another trepidation to avoid. Now that you are free of all of these negative thought patterns, you can enjoy social interaction with a head held high and nothing to apologize for. Another key benefit that you may not have seen or realized before, is that doing something nice for others simply feels good. You are able to emphasize the happiness of others. Seeing a smile on another person's face that you have caused can feel so rewarding in ways that you have never felt before! Even for more selfish reasons, it feels good, as in the sense of being the hero of someone's day. It is a wholesome feeling. It is a feeling that is entirely guilt-free. Some examples of positive social outings would be simple activities like volunteer work or attending or even participating in sports events. Maybe your place of employment has a softball league, or your colleagues enjoy disc golf. These are activities that directly give back to your community or peer group. These are higher levels of commitment, so if you are not ready for that quite yet, maybe you could try something a little less structured. Meeting trusted friends in a relaxed social environment could be a little bit more comfortable for you. Invite a friend, or a few friends, out for lunch or to a store of your common interests. This kind of setting makes for a good conversation that is not so personal if you are not ready for that. It is perfectly acceptable to take your time developing your social identity, as this step is very important. Meeting friends in this kind of setting can also help you learn more about your friends and even yourself! Maybe they have an interest that you did not even know that you had! Maybe you have a friend who is very interested in tabletop gaming, which might be an area of interest that you have never explored! Your friends and new interests will most likely lead you to new friends and even more positive and interesting activities. It is easy to get sucked into the positive life; all you have to do is take the first step!

Working within your comfortable level of commitment is essential, but it is also important to actually engage in these or similar activities. The goal of this section is to establish new positive habits to replace self-destructive habits. Just like how picking up and reading this book was a crucial first step, this is another crucial step. Do not fret though! This step is easier than what you would think. Most of the time, the fear associated with the activity is much worse than the actual activity, and you should know how to properly process negative thought patterns. All you have to do is breathe and take that step. Your friends, family, and colleagues will be more than happy to have you included.

It is important to establish positive relationships that engage in positive activities. It is also important to allow yourself to learn what positive social activities are. A common misconception, reinforced by advertisements and common television shows, is that all social activity takes place with alcohol. That is simply not true. In fact, the most productive and happiest people may rarely step foot in one of these establishments. As a side note, you may also be surprised at the money you save when you do not frequently visit these establishments, which brings me back to advertisements. That is why those media outlets pursue that lifestyle; it is purely to promote a lifestyle that will earn their company more money. In that respect, establish your own idea of happiness! Find out what it is that truly makes you happy! You are most likely to find that engaging with friends develops real bonds and promotes honest happiness. You are most likely to find that volunteer work, or even saying yes when someone asks for a favor, is more fulfilling than anything that you have experienced in your previous life.

You should feel proud of yourself for taking this step! Now that you are taking steps to not only better yourself, but to solidify and reinforce it with positive social activities, there is nothing that can get in your way on your path to being happier, more wholesome you! Once again, congratulations!

Chapter 8: How DBT Has Enhanced Your Life

Although this book has seemed to have an almost conversational flow, it has actually followed very closely to the five functions of DBT. As this book has mentioned before, the goal of this is not to assume an authoritative role over you, the reader. This book was designed to reinforce your own choices and merely give examples of positive living for those who may be unaware or fearful of how to live as such. Having said that, it is now time to relate what we have learned to the five functions of Dialectical Behavior Therapy. Before we do that, let's define what those five functions are.

- Enhance client's capabilities
- Improve the client's motivation
- Assure generalization to the client's natural environment
- Structure the environment
- Enhance the therapist's capabilities and support their motivation

The clinical way to go about enhancing your capabilities is to reinforce the skills of DBT. We have used many skills directly from the actual standard of DBT, such as the acronyms DEAR MAN, FAST, and PLEASE MASTER. These are acronyms that you would become familiar with if you were to attend a regular DBT session. We have also discussed important skills like practicing mindfulness and emotional regulation. These are also skills that you are most likely to encounter in an actual DBT session. This book has taken those lessons and broken them down for you to study, practice, and make into your own at your own pace by your own choices. Using these skills in your own life will only work to enhance the quality of your life and introduce you to lifestyles that mirror your interests, even those that you may not be aware that you have. This is an exciting time to be alive, and an exciting time for you!

The next function of DBT is the enhancement of the client's motivation. This book was designed to keep you motivated throughout, but it is not what was written or the speed in which you read it. The real motivation comes from you. You have rewarded yourself for picking up this book and sticking to it all the way to the end. By now, you deserve to have developed a sense of pride in making these positive changes in your life! There is no outside force that can motivate you to the extent that you can motivate yourself.

This book was written to be a companion to your own life. You are free to read or not read, follow or not follow, at your own pace. The fact that you have made it this far is something to be celebrated. It shows that you are honest in your desire to rid yourself of negative thought processes and self-destructive habits. There is not a single person or entity that is able to instill that level of motivation inside of you. You have shown that you are committed; not to this book or these processes, but you are committed to yourself. You have already taken better care of yourself than previously you might have thought possible. It is not only acceptable but appropriate to celebrate yourself at this time. This is a real achievement that you have accomplished, and one that many people take multiple tries to achieve. Some may not ever get to the level of clarity and health that you have already achieved for yourself. Once again, Congratulations!

The third function of DBT may seem confusing at first. It is to assure generalization to the client's natural environment. What that means is that this treatment, and this book, is designed to be a companion piece to live alongside without overtaking your life. This is not a program designed to put your life on hold. The effectiveness of this is that it promotes ease of transition into your new lifestyle while giving examples that are digestible by you because they relate to you, just as you are. It is easy to take this book with you and read it at your own pace or use the skills you have learned through a DBT session or in this book while you go about living your day-to-day life. There is no commitment besides the commitment that you have made to yourself and are comfortable with.

In an actual DBT session, they would address this function within the moment coaching. You would have access to a 24/7 phone number that you would be encouraged to call if you are having a hard time with applying the lessons to your life you would have learned during a session. This is an excellent tool, and if you were to attend a DBT session, I would strongly encourage you to feel free to use it. These coaches are not there to judge your choices. They understand the material and are also encouraged to process emotions without judgment. This is purely for the benefit of you! It is also encouraging to have outside motivation when your motivation might be hitting a low point. There is nothing to worry about though, just like the inevitability of sickness or negative thoughts, you cannot fault yourself for when your motivation is feeling weaker at the moment. Just relax, call that number, and celebrate yourself for making the positive choice at that moment when you may not have previously.

We are almost through the list here, I hope that you feel encouraged to continue. The fourth function of DBT is to structure the client's environment. This one can seem almost scary because you have gone this far along your own choices. There is nothing to fear though because this step is not designed to take away your choices, merely to help you and provide tools for you to make positive choices when you may not have previously. How a DBT session would go about doing that would be to assign you a case manager. This is someone who is dedicated to your case and is working with you to ensure your success.

An important aspect of this function is the thought process when accepting it. It is not there to control your lifestyle. When a client has made poor life choices and made a habit out of them, then they might not be aware of or be comfortable with lifestyle choices that are more positive and sustainable. You have already decided to live a positive life, now it is time to learn how. That is the purpose of this function. In DBT, there is a strong focus on replacing negative habits with more positive habits. This is because pure motivation has to be outwardly expressed and used for it to continue. Imagine your positive motivation as a match. You can light the match, and it will burn for a while. It is hot, it is bright. It has the potential to continue on, but it can only continue on if fuel is introduced to the match. Imagine this function of DBT as a pile of wood arranged for you in a fire pit, ready to be lit by your motivational match. Once you apply the match to the wood in the fire pit, then the fire burns much longer in a safe environment. Your motivation must be applied to a positive atmosphere to continue on. Your case manager or other individuals in your DBT session use this function to safely provide you with those structured, positive environments. Go forth and do well for yourself and others!

Have you made it this far? I hope that you have because this is now the final function of Dialectical Behavior Therapy. That function is to enhance the therapist's capabilities and support their motivation. DBT therapists work in a team to more effectively enhance the lives and understanding of their clients. This is important for the team as well as the client. A typical DBT team meeting may start with a mindfulness exercise, reading of the previous minutes, and then discuss strategies to further their treatment. It is important for you to be engaging and helpful along with your therapist as this whole treatment only works with your commitment. An example of this would be to imagine you and your therapist on a rowboat. Your therapist will not be able to motivate you to continue to row if they are not participating in the work. Your therapist can also not row by themselves if you are not helping. This whole style of treatment is designed to be a cooperative endeavor. You should feel excited and encouraged to participate. The end result will be a happier, more positive you!

This chapter is here to serve the purpose of relating what you have learned to the structured skills that are discussed in an actual Dialectical Behavior Therapy session. It is strongly encouraged that you attend these sessions and take what you have learned in this book with you to those sessions. There is nothing that you should not be able to achieve in this aspect of your life between this book, those sessions, and your own motivation! You have a threefold angle of attack on your negative habits that you wish to eradicate from your life. Finding a DBT session is easy, as it is a growing style of treatment. Everyone involved wishes only the best of success for you! Continue on with your own choices and feel proud of how far you have come!

9 781913 710217